The End of the
ROARING TWENTIES
Prohibition and Repeal

From 1920 to 1933, it was against federal law to manufacture or sell alcoholic beverages in the United States. Religious, moral and medical opposition to alcohol had existed from the time of the Pilgrims, and such 19th-century groups as the Women's Christian Temperance Union and individuals like the hatchet-wielding Carry Nation made the movement nationwide. When the Prohibition Amendment was passed, the victory of the anti-liquor cause seemed complete; but people would not obey the law, and illegal liquor gave birth to an era of crime and violence. Even as rural morality had triumphed in the legislatures, the dominant patterns of American life had become urban. The flavor and follies of the roaring twenties were ended by the Great Depression, and Prohibition was finally repealed. This account of the rise and fall of Prohibition is social history at its most engrossing.

D1316804

The End of the
ROARING TWENTIES
Prohibition and Repeal

BY BILL SEVERN

Illustrated with Photographs

**Julian Messner
New York** Ⓜ

Published simultaneously in the United States and Canada by
Julian Messner, a division of Simon & Schuster, Inc., 1 West 39
Street, New York, N.Y. 10018. All rights reserved.

Printed in the United States of America

Library of Congress Catalog Card No. 73-79698

The End of the
ROARING TWENTIES
Prohibition and Repeal

1

Some of the roar of the 1920s came from the tommy guns of rival criminal gangs, from the rumble of trucks smuggling liquor across the borders and from the chugging of boats running in rum from the seas. It was in the gurgle of hip flasks, the tinkle of bottles and glasses in speakeasies, the bubbling of illegal stills and the jingle of money to bribe police and politicians. But even louder was the roar that divided the nation in argument over whether the federal government should go on trying to police the drinking habits of the people.

Most Americans had been solidly in favor of prohibition when the Eighteenth Amendment to the Constitution went into effect in 1920. Twelve years later, most Americans were ready to admit it had been a failure. Born of an honest desire for law and order, to meet evils that had troubled America from its beginnings, prohibition had become an economic, political, religious and geographical issue. It involved the growing pains of a nation shifting from farms to industries, and the conflict between rural and city areas and between those who clung to simple old-fashioned codes and those who revolted against the strict Puritanism of the past.

Enacted during an era of Spartan faith in national virtue that reached its emotional peak in World War I, prohibition seemed to offer the promise of a great cure-all for poverty, corruption and crime. America, victorious in the "war that was to end all wars," had been in no mood for halfway measures, and prohibition fitted the noble belief that enforced virtue would solve all problems and bring everlasting prosperity and happiness. It was part of the golden dream of a national age of innocence.

But that age was fading even as the Eighteenth Amendment went into effect. War itself shattered many illusions, and the changes that followed brought rebellion against the patterns of the past. Resisted, mocked and disobeyed by millions who regarded it as an invasion of personal liberty, prohibition failed its promises and brought evils of its own. It was part of the Constitution and the basic law of the land, but without the willing support of the people no law could be enforced in a democracy, and prohibition never was.

Disgust for it grew slowly through the most lawless decade America had ever known. The Great Depression finally crushed the good-time boom, and a suddenly sobered nation, desperately searching for some way out of its despair, became determined by 1932 to overturn that part of the Constitution and sweep prohibition out the door.

The prohibitionists, who had been in supreme power four years before, found themselves without any place to go after the national party conventions in June, 1932. Republicans demanded drastic changes in prohibition, and Democrats demanded outright repeal. Franklin D. Roosevelt told the convention of wildly cheering Democrats who nominated him as their presidential candidate: "From this date on, the Eighteenth Amendment is doomed!"

In the November elections of 1932, the mandate of the voters was as overwhelmingly for repeal as it was for the rest of the New Deal. Although newly elected President Roosevelt would not take office until the following March, congress moved almost immediately. With debate under way on a resolution for a Twenty-first Amendment that would cancel the Eighteenth, prohibition began its death march in the senate early in February, 1933.

Senator Morris Sheppard of Texas, honored by the drys through the years of prohibition as the "father of the Eighteenth Amendment," took to the senate floor to stage a one-man filibuster against repeal. But he spoke for what he knew was a dying cause. Waiting at the senate door was the repeal resolution.

It was one-thirty in the afternoon by the gold watch he pulled from his pocket and laid on his paper-cluttered desk when Senator Sheppard cleared his throat and began talking. He meant to talk about anything and everything for as long as he could to keep the resolution from reaching the floor. A small, prim, gray-haired man, he began discussing the proceedings of the League of Nations and monotonously recited its history. He turned to reading old documents, long columns of figures and reports, in the hope that other dry senators would join him and start a full filibuster. His dronings drove most of his fellow senators from the chamber. Vice-President Charles Curtis seemed nearly asleep at the rostrum.

Late in the afternoon, another senator interrupted Sheppard to ask how long he meant to go on. "That depends on

9

how long the spirit moves me," Sheppard said. "I can't tell how long I may speak when I am under the inspiration of a sense of duty. It may be indefinitely. I can hold out."

He did go on until ten o'clock that night. But no others joined him. Abruptly then, he put his watch back into his pocket and sat down. The next day the senate voted to take up the repeal resolution; during the two days of debate that followed, Senator Sheppard had no more to say.

The senate debate was no longer over whether the Eighteenth Amendment should be repealed, but how that repeal should be carried out. Drys tried to salvage what they could by seeking some federal controls, but wets swept the restrictions aside. On February 16, all debate ended. A hush fell over the senate, and Vice-President Curtis announced: "The question now is, shall the joint resolution pass?" The clerk began reading the names as the roll call started.

Up in the gallery with other dry leaders who had fought the last battle for public opinion was Mrs. Ella Boole, head of the Woman's Christian Temperance Union. There were no cheers or boos as the count of votes went on, only tense silence. At last, Vice-President Curtis intoned: "On this question, the yeas are 63, the nays are 23. More than two-thirds having voted in the affirmative, the joint resolution is passed."

Mrs. Boole sat down hard, with tears in her eyes. On the senate floor below, there was cheering. The demonstration lasted five minutes.

Four days later, with only a half-hour of final debate, the House approved the Senate resolution 289 to 121, after New York Representative Emanuel Celler had urged, "Let us flee from prohibition as one would from a foul dungeon." And Congressman Fiorello La Guardia, soon to be New York City's mayor, said, "We are now too weary . . . to celebrate our victory."

The proposed Twenty-first Amendment to the Constitution, repealing the Eighteenth, was sent on its way to the states, where the battles of ratification would be fought, not by the legislatures but by a convention elected in each state solely for that purpose.

National prohibition, produced by a century of moral and religious crusades to which thousands of men and women had dedicated their lives, born of years of battles in the cities and in the states, was about to end. Noble though it was in purpose, it had multiplied bootleggers, speakeasies, bribery and corruption, lawlessness and organized crime.

But all those things also had existed in connection with the liquor trade long before the Eighteenth Amendment. The problems of the demon rum had troubled America through history and even before the United States began. The roar that became so loud in the 1920s started centuries before.

2

Prohibition was first tried in America to protect colonial settlers from the attacks of Indians who were inflamed by the "strong waters" the settlers themselves had taught them to drink. Massachusetts and other early colonies enacted stiff prohibition laws to forbid the sale or gift of liquor to the Indians. But colonial authorities found the Indian prohibition laws almost impossible to enforce.

Enterprising traders bootlegged liquor to the Indians and shrewdly used it to bargain for furs and other things of value. Ambitious landseekers discovered that liquor helped overcome Indian resistance to giving up choice tracts of property and rich stands of timber. Important merchants claimed that Indian prohibition interfered with the development of colonial commerce. Restrictions gradually were lifted or ignored.

The effect on the Indians was tragic. Colonial literature

was filled with denunciations of greedy traders who got Indians drunk to trick them and rob them. But few settlers wanted prohibition to protect the Indians, even though they wanted strict curbs on Indian drunkenness and disorders.

The colonists themselves, including the stern Puritans, considered alcoholic beverages among the necessities of life when used in moderation. They often referred to liquor as "the good creature of God" and for the most part had no thought of prohibiting their own enjoyment of drink. Colonial authorities encouraged the making and selling of beer, wine and liquor, not only to satisfy their needs but to produce tax revenue to maintain forts and to build schools and churches. Brewing and distilling were among the first important American industries, and they provided profits that expanded other colonial commerce.

The first ships to reach the New World carried alcoholic beverages as a vital part of their provisions. The good ship *Arabella,* which brought John Winthrop to the Massachusetts colony as governor in 1630, had aboard "42 tuns of beer, 14 tuns of water," and the ratio of three drinks of beer to one of water was about average for pioneer voyagers.

But while most colonists approved moderate drinking, the man or woman who drank too much was a social outcast, and the habitual drunkard faced severe punishment. Misuse of any of the "good things of nature" was considered a sin. Normal drinking was as much accepted as eating, but if a drinker couldn't control his thirst the law was determined to do it for him.

In all the colonies, drunks were fined, sentenced to the stocks, sent to the whipping stool or ordered to wear the scarlet letter "D" for "Drunkard" about their necks for up to a year. Laborers, servants and slaves usually were more severely punished than men of property. For a poor man to get drunk was not only a sin against society but also against his employer, since he was wasting time that might be spent at useful work.

Regulations were intended to control the use of liquor, not to prohibit it. But the tavern keeper who failed to obey them was likely to have his place closed. Drinking hours were limited, and usually there was a limit to the amount of liquor a person was allowed to drink at any one sitting. In many places he was forbidden to dance, sing or indulge in loud talk or boisterous behavior. Some colonies had informers check on conduct in the taverns, and official lists were made of those who were denied the right to purchase drinks.

Where regulations were so severe that they began to interfere with the common pleasures of drinking, the first speakeasies sprang up, frequented by those who wanted to drink as much as they pleased when they pleased, free of official snooping. Unlicensed and often thoroughly disreputable, they became breeding places of crime. Colonial legislatures and town officials issued warning proclamations and adopted laws to prohibit them, but the early speakeasies continued to flourish.

As the colonial governments increased import duties and excise taxes on liquor to raise revenues, smuggling, rum-running and moonshining grew. Colonial revenue men were few. Smuggling was comparatively easy, and those who tried to evade the duties and taxes were many. Some colonies appointed special customs officers to search ships and warehouses and to seize illegal imports. But in most areas enforcement was up to regular constables, who were busy with other duties and who frequently sympathized with the law evaders. Many otherwise law-abiding colonial citizens objected to such taxes as government interference with private business, and people strongly resented the revenue snooping of spies and informers.

Rum changed the drinking habits of the colonies in the

late 1600s as New England developed trade with the British West Indies. As thirst for the satisfying West Indian beverage grew, New England's distillers started to make their own cheap rum by importing the necessary molasses from the Indies. Before long it was enormously popular in all the colonies, and rum drinking became a general habit that penetrated every level of colonial life.

Rhode Island was the first big rum-distilling center, but there were important distillers in other parts of New England, as well as in New York, Pennsylvania and the Carolinas, who distributed their products throughout the colonies. Some sent traveling salesmen into the cities and hawkers to travel by wagon through rural districts. Stills multiplied until hardly any large town was without at least one rum-maker of its own.

In 1723 some Rhode Island merchants turned the use of rum to the notorious slave trade. French brandy had long been used in trading for ivory, gold and slaves along the African coast, but the New Englanders substituted the much cheaper rum. By the mid-1700s Newport and Providence had become the chief bases for the trade, but other parts of New England soon were engaged in what became a triangle of riches upon which much of the early prosperity of the colonies was founded. New England rum was readily exchanged for slaves at the African slave-trading stations. Traders then sold the slaves and invested profits in West Indian molasses. The molasses was sold in turn to the New England distillers to make more rum to satisfy the thirst of the colonies.

In Rhode Island alone, during a ten-year period, more than one hundred vessels were built to engage in the trade. Traffic was so heavy at times that one trader reported nineteen competing rum ships at a single slave station on the Guinea Coast in 1736. At the height of the trade, New

Englanders were exchanging an estimated 600,000 gallons of rum a year for slaves, some of which were traded for as little as three gallons each. But as rum became more plentiful, competition increased and the value of slaves went up. The trade of liquor finally became unprofitable, and New Englanders gradually began to turn from the slave business to put their rum profits into other lines of commerce.

The flood of rum, meanwhile, had spilled into nearly every American home and was generally accepted as a great boon to mankind. Beer, wine and other liquors, including the cider so cheaply made from plentiful apples, gave way to rum, and its popularity lasted in many of the colonies even after the large-scale distilling of corn and rye whiskey began. Rum was considered a tonic for good health and a general household remedy for all ailments. Parents spoon-fed it to children, and mothers gave it to fretful infants to hush their crying.

People drank it at funerals, weddings, christenings, at town meetings, council gatherings and most community affairs, whether the occasion was festive or solemn. When neighbors gathered to clear woods or fields, to help a man harvest his crop, raise his house or put up his barn, rum was served to lubricate the labor. The clergy drank it liberally, along with everyone else, when ceremonies were held to open a new church, install new pews, or ordain ministers. It was the common beverage of rich and poor alike, both sexes and all ages, and the total abstainer was a rare exception.

But among the colonies, Georgia was an exception by law. It was there that the first real attempt was made to enforce prohibition in America. Georgia's founding father, James Oglethorpe, was also the father of prohibition. When Oglethorpe led his first band of carefully chosen colonists to Georgia in 1733, he was determined to create a sober

17

society that would shun the excessive use of hard liquor. His views were shared by the other English Trustees of the Georgia colony. They supplied him with a hundred copies of *Dr. Hale's Friendly Admonition to the Drinkers of Brandy*, which advocated the use of beer instead of other alcoholic beverages.

But the new colonists had hardly settled in what was to become Savannah before some began to make rum instead of beer. They soon began importing more rum from South Carolina. Oglethorpe wrote the Trustees about the poor conditions in the struggling colony and blamed much of the trouble on heavy drinking.

The Londoners answered with a call for prohibition: "As it appears by your letters that the sickness among the people is owing to the excessive drinking of rum punch, the Trustees do absolutely forbid their drinking, or even having any rum, and agree with you so entirely in your sentiments that they order all rum that shall be brought there to be immediately staved."

Georgians paid little attention to the letter of prohibition, so the Trustees got the British Parliament and King George II to put the full force of law behind it. The King approved an act that flatly prohibited the import or sale of rum in Georgia. It went into effect in 1735 and was almost totally disobeyed. The attempt to enforce it produced, on a smaller scale, many of the conditions that were to make the 1920s roar nearly two centuries later.

Community leaders as well as average citizens looked upon Georgia's colonial prohibition with ridicule and contempt. There were no effective controls and not enough manpower to police violations, and public sympathy was more on the side of the lawbreakers than the enforcers. Illegal stills operated in back-country areas, and colonial agents who tried to track down the first moonshiners met a hostile reception. Rum-runners brought their boats in from South Carolina to land cargoes in secluded coves. Others carried heavy kegs of rum by foot or horseback over wilderness trails. There were fights between rival bootleggers and hijacking attempts by bands that tried to steal the rum while it was being taken to towns and villages. Posing as ordinary peddlers, bootleggers traveled the country roads. In the settlements, speakeasies flourished in huts, back rooms of stores and private homes.

A representative of the Trustees, William Stephens, reported that no square mile of London had more illegal tippling houses than some parts of Georgia. Many of them, he warned, were rapidly becoming "nurseries of villainy," where outlaws gathered, laborers idled and profanity filled the air with curses against both God and the colonial government. Settlers were neglecting the business of the colony to spend their time chasing rum, and officials were being corrupted with bribes.

Others complained to the Trustees that prohibition was making a mockery of the court system. Rum-runners and bootleggers, when caught, demanded trial by jury, and their fellow citizens simply refused to convict them, no matter what the evidence. Oglethorpe himself, although he strongly supported enforcement, sadly admitted that there probably weren't twelve men in all of Georgia who would convict anyone for selling rum.

Convinced that prohibition could not be enforced against the public will, the Trustees in 1742 finally gave up the experiment. They permitted imports of rum again and put into effect a system of licensing taverns and public houses. The pioneer rum-runners, bootleggers and speakeasies soon faded out of business.

In the rest of the colonies, where prohibition never was tried, rum also brought troubles. Taverns multiplied and regulations eased, and licenses often were granted through political influence rather than to men of high character. Drunkenness, idling, rough conduct and disrespect for authority became common. Towns which once had looked upon the tavern as a boon to the community began to consider it an evil.

But rum was still the key to colonial prosperity, vital to trade and to the development of commerce, and its manufacture, sale and use were highly approved by most people as the colonies struggled to become a nation.

3

The soldiers of Revolution in George Washington's ragged army at Valley Forge during the terrible winter of 1777–78 complained of "no pay, no clothes, no provisions, no rum." Many considered the lack of rum as great an ordeal as the lack of food. Rum was thought to be necessary to supplement the meager food supply, to preserve good health, to ward off winter chills and "to keep body and soul together." The ration was a half-pint a day, but soldiers seldom got it.

War cut off trade with the West Indies, halting both imports of good rum and the molasses needed to make domestic rum. Shortages became acute. Profiteering was widespread, and the government appealed to all patriotic citizens to sell their liquor to the Army. Whiskey gradually became a popular substitute for rum, not only in the Army but among civilians, and it grew to rival rum and finally to replace it as the favorite national drink.

21

Farmers, first in frontier Western Pennsylvania and then in other places, distilled whiskey on their farms from crops of rye and corn. City distilleries then began to operate, and whiskey drinking grew so much during the Revolution that, instead of a shortage of liquor, there soon was a threatened shortage of grain for bread. Some alarmists feared that whiskey-making might cause a national famine. The Continental Congress, meeting in Philadelphia, unanimously adopted a resolution in 1777 that became the first official attempt by the new government of the United States to control the flow of liquor. It resolved "that it be recommended to the several Legislatures in the United States immediately to pass laws the most effective for putting an immediate stop to the pernicious practice of distilling grain, by which the most extensive evils are likely to be derived if not quickly prevented."

Pennsylvania and New Jersey were among states that adopted strict laws to limit the amount of grain converted to whiskey, but with little effect. The government was too weak to enforce its recommendations, and people fiercely defended their right to individual liberty, especially in habits of drink. Whiskey was the main cash crop upon which many farmers depended for a living. Readily salable, the concentrated product of the farms was easier to transport over poor roads than were bulky loads of grain. In some sections it became a substitute for money itself, with prices of all other commodities figured in terms of their value in barrels of whiskey.

After the Revolution, a liquor tax became the first means the hard-pressed new federal government turned to for raising funds. In its first session under the Constitution, the first tariff bill of congress in 1789 put a tax on all imported alcoholic beverages and on the molasses for making rum. Secretary of the Treasury Alexander Hamilton supported the tax, but Secretary of State Thomas Jefferson, soon to become Hamilton's direct political enemy, was against it and called it "an infernal tax." Two years later, Hamilton got congress to put a tax not only on imports but also on American manufacture of whiskey, and the uproar led to an armed rebellion.

Many condemned the direct federal tax on corn and rye whiskey and on the stills that made it as an act to impose government standards of morality. "If any man supposes that a mere law can turn the taste of a people from ardent spirits," said Congressman Fisher Ames of Massachusetts, "he has a romantic notion of legislative power."

Hardest hit by the new liquor tax were frontiersmen and farmers of Pennsylvania and back-country Virginia, many of whom were to become Jefferson's followers in the political revolution of 1800 that was to make him president. They had many grievances for which they blamed the aristocratic Federalists, and the liquor tax seemed to them just one more discrimination against the common man. The frontiersmen took to arms against the politicians in Washington who wanted to cut the profits of the stills that were on nearly every farm.

Men who had fought in the Revolution defiantly raised the Liberty Poles again, held mass meetings and loaded their guns to fight off the revenue agents of the new federal government with the battle cry: "Liberty and no excise!" They tarred and feathered some revenue men, drove off others with shotgun blasts, attacked a federal marshal and burned the home of a regional tax inspector. Mobs destroyed the stills of those who paid taxes and took armed possession of several towns. The whole Pennsylvania countryside joined in what became known as the Whiskey Rebellion.

Hamilton, persuaded President Washington to call up the militia of three states and personally went with the over-

23

whelming force of 15,000 soldiers who slogged their way through rain and mud over the mountains to put down the insurrection. The rebellion collapsed without major bloodshed. The frontiersmen finally gave in and agreed to pay the tax, and the government gained new authority by demonstrating that it could enforce the laws of congress. But the war over whiskey, which Jefferson deplored as an unnecessary show of federal force, strengthened frontier hatred for the Federalists and gained Jefferson great popular support.

Americans, meanwhile, were downing a staggering amount of whiskey. Liquor was considered so beneficial for health and good spirits that many men and women seldom went without a drink for more than a few hours. A good ration of spirits was included as part of the set wages of nearly every workman. The employer who didn't provide his men with whiskey was considered cruel, and the farmer who didn't supply his hands with plenty of liquor found it hard to get help. Grocers and merchants kept whiskey barrels on tap for customers, and the traveler going almost anywhere was never far from a place that could satisfy his thirst. Whiskey was taken internally by both men and women for almost every ailment, accident or disease, and what wasn't swallowed was rubbed on as an external linament.

The plight of the drunkard and his family, often reduced to poverty and disgrace, was known to everyone and became a common concern. It was to protect the home from troubles caused by those who couldn't control their drinking habits that the first informal temperance movements began. More and more clergymen took to their pulpits to urge moderation.

But the most influential early spokesman for temperance was not a clergyman, but a man of science, Dr. Benjamin Rush. Born in Philadelphia about 1745, Rush was fifteen when he graduated from the College of New Jersey at

Princeton and decided to make medicine his career. He completed his training in Europe under some of the outstanding medical men of the time, got his degree from the University of Edinburgh and returned to the United States in 1769 to become the first professor of chemistry in the American colonies and later the University of Pennsylvania's first professor of medicine. One of the patriot plotters of the Revolution, a member of congress and a signer of the Declaration of Independence, Rush was named Physician-General of the Continental Army.

He took charge of troop hospitals at a time when there was desperate need to conserve fighting manpower and came to the conclusion that heavy drinking was destroying the effective fighting ability of more American soldiers than British weapons ever would. Rush made a long and continuing study of the effects of intemperance and decided its greatest cause was the false view the general public had of alcohol as a health tonic and medicinal cure-all.

As the Army's Physician-General, he published his *Directions for Preserving the Health of Soldiers* in 1778, warning troops under his care against excessive use of hard liquor. In it, he tried to refute the commonly held belief that liquor relieved fatigue, sustained hard labor and protected a man against heat and cold, fevers, and other camp diseases. His advice was too radical to have much effect on Army policy, but it did start others questioning the supposed health-giving benefits of liquor.

When he retired from the Army after the victory of the Revolution, Rush made the subject part of the scientific research to which he devoted himself. As a medical scientist he was interested chiefly in the then almost unexplored field of the relationship between mind and body. Among the first to advance the theory that mental illnesses often could be traced to diseases of the body and that the reverse also was true, his studies all touched in some degree on the intemperate use of liquor. He became increasingly convinced that heavy drinking was a medical, moral and social evil, and that the whole public needed to be educated about it.

In 1784 he published a pamphlet that was to change the thinking of thousands of Americans, influence others for years to come and inspire the real start of the temperance movement in the United States. In its forty closely printed pages, his *Inquiry into the Effects of Spirituous Liquors on the Human Body and Mind* contained the first comprehensive, scientific and carefully documented attack against the use of alcohol. It was so compelling in its conclusions and so ably written that it became the fundamental temperance text. Coming as it did at a time of national mood for reform, it gained immediate popularity.

Editions were exhausted as fast as they came from the press, and the demand continued for thirty years. Excerpts were printed in dozens of papers, periodicals and almanacs. Each year at harvest time, copies were distributed to farmers in the hope that they would stop including liquor as part of the day's pay for farm hands. Others went to ministers of all faiths and to editors, factory owners and public officials. Long after Rush died, his *Inquiry* was still being read and copied by other temperance speakers and writers.

In his *Inquiry*, Rush attacked the common belief that hard liquors were a good supplement to the diet and said they had no food value at all. He argued that instead of improving health they aggravated most diseases and were the cause of many. A man who substituted moderate quantities of wine and beer, he said, might look forward to a long happy life, but the man who drank whiskey and rum might become a confirmed sot who was no better than an animal. "In folly," he wrote, "it causes him to resemble a calf; in stupidity, an ass; in roaring, a mad bull; in quarreling and fighting, a dog; in cruelty, a tiger; in fetor, a skunk; in filthiness, a hog; in obscenity, a he-goat."

He gained many converts. Merchants wrote him that they were halting the sale of whiskey and rum. Some farmers and factory owners promised they would supply no more liquor rations to their workers. There were distillers who voluntarily shut their plants and went out of business and tavern keepers who decided they would sell only wine and beer. Church leaders responded, and in a number of communities citizens got together and formed informal temperance groups, pledging themselves to abstain from ardent spirits.

Rush was so encouraged that before his death in 1813 he predicted the day when everybody would shun rum and whiskey entirely as a matter of self-control and in a patriotic desire to produce a healthy and happy America. Actually the great majority of Americans went on drinknig as much or more than before, but Benjamin Rush had inspired a crusading minority to organize what was to become a never-ending fight to achieve his temperance utopia.

4

A small-town country doctor in upstate New York, Dr. Billy J. Clark, had been worried over the heavy drinking among farmers and lumberjacks in his area, and when he read Dr. Benjamin Rush's famous essay in 1808, he became convinced something had to be done. He was so alarmed by what he read that he saddled up a horse, rode through a cold March night to the home of his minister and burst in upon the startled clergyman to shout: "We're becoming a town of drunkards, and we've got to do something to stop it!"

They talked over the problem, and the result was what was probably America's first organized temperance society. Led by Dr. Clark, some forty of the most important men in town met in a schoolhouse on April 30, 1808, to organize the Union Temperance Society of Moreau and Northumberland. They adopted the first written temperance constitution and by-laws, pledged themselves to abstain from drinking "any distilled spirits" as a one-year experiment and hoped their example would lead others to question the habits of drink.

Newspapers picked up the story and made a joke of it, claiming that without liquor there would be no husking of corn, other farm work would go undone, houses would not be built and even quilting bees and weddings would suffer from a drying up of spirits. There were more serious charges that Dr. Clark was threatening public health by coaxing people to give up alcohol, which nearly everybody believed was necessary to ward off disease.

But the society grew in membership, and at the end of the test year there was a big public meeting that gained wide publicity. Members enthusiastically stepped forward to testify, one after another, to the benefits of abstinence. News of the successful experiment spread, and other communities were encouraged to copy the plan. Dozens of little temperance clubs began to organize throughout New York and the New England states, and then in the South and the Midwest. Their number gradually grew to hundreds, some of them state-wide in membership.

Another man, who was to have far greater influence on the beginning temperance movement, the Reverend Lyman Beecher, also read Dr. Benjamin Rush's essay on the effects of alcohol and found that it "fermented in my mind." Born in New Haven in 1775, he was taught by his parents that liquor was evil and drinking a sin, and was shocked as a student at Yale to discover heavy drinking among his classmates, and even more dismayed when he became a clergyman and saw fellow ministers line up for drinks at church meetings.

As pastor of a church at Litchfield, Connecticut, he decided that the clergy, as well as the public, needed a reform of morals. Beecher worked to ban liquor from church assemblies, to get church members to give up any interest they had in its manufacture or sale and to form voluntary associations of churchgoers to seek strick enforcement of liquor control laws.

In 1813 he became head of the Connecticut Society for the Reformation of Morals, an organization that included not only distinguished clergymen but also many of the state's most important citizens, men of wealth, political power and social prestige. Dedicated to arousing public opinion to "save the moral fibre of the nation" from destruction by "rum-selling, tippling folk, infidels and ruff-scruff," the group sought to put an end to the laxity which allowed "drunkards to reel through the streets day after day and year after year with entire impunity."

In other American cities reform groups grew on the conditions that followed the War of 1812. Poverty, crime and drunkenness were on the rise, and temperance reforms enlisted overburdened charity organizations in the cause and won the support of civic authorities, who were faced with a breakdown of law enforcement. They also gained the political backing of those who feared an uprising of the common people against the aristocracy of wealth, prestige and privilege represented by the established churches. The movement coincided with a great national religious revival that began to sweep the country, and temperance became part of the accepted work of the churches, carried on with a zealous missionary spirit by those who considered drink the worst obstacle to leading sinners to salvation.

A flood of published sermons, pamphlets and articles appeared. Among the most popular were the writings of the Reverend Mason Locke Weems, Episcopal clergyman, traveling bookseller and hack writer for religious publications. His chief claim to fame was the authorship of a highly fictionalized biography of George Washington, in which he invented the myth about Washington's boyhood refusal to tell a lie after chopping down a cherry tree. Parson Weems wrote a booklet in 1812, *The Drunkard's Looking Glass*, that offered his "Golden Receipts" against drunkenness. It included such advice as a warning that men should avoid fighting duels because even if they were successful, "nine times in ten the memory of the murdered drives the murderer to the bottle."

On a more serious level, Lyman Beecher in the fall of 1825 preached the first of a series of sermons to his Litchfield congregation that were to become the new basic text of the temperance movement. They were even more important in arousing national public opinion against liquor than Rush's *Inquiry* had been in its time. Published the next year, his *Six Sermons on the Nature, Occasions, Signs, Evils and Remedy of Intemperance* ran through five editions in as many months and kept printing presses busy for the next ten years.

Reprinted by temperance groups, constantly quoted in newspapers and magazines and by public speakers, they inspired the writing of thousands of other talks and sermons. Beecher's convincing appeals to the deepest emotions of religious belief, health, human happiness and the desire for prosperity and profit and national pride in community and government stirred the country toward reform as nothing else had. His *Six Sermons* vividly portrayed the evils of drink, called for "banishment of ardent spirits from the list of lawful articles of commerce" and regarded intemperance as a physical disease which had its beginnings in the germs of moderate drinking and for which he claimed the only practical remedy was immediate and total abstinence.

Wandering missionaries echoed his words everywhere, from large auditoriums and city churches to the smallest log-cabin meeting places of the frontier West. The personal crusaders, backed by the pulpit and by printed appeals, enlarged little temperance societies into state and county groups with many branches. Pioneer settlers, moving into new areas, carried with them the temperance lessons they had learned at home.

Beecher, meanwhile, was called in 1826 from his small Connecticut parish to Boston's important Hanover Street Church, where he drew enormous and enthusiastic crowds. In Boston, he gave much of his time to a movement already under way to form a national temperance society which would unite all the small groups across the country.

Its prime mover was another Boston clergyman, the Reverend Justin Edwards, who brought together sixteen of the most distinguished men in Massachusetts on February 13, 1826, to establish the American Society for the Promotion of Temperance. Edwards became its first full-time secretary and in the next ten years built the society into a nationwide organization of one million members.

Probably as much as any other individual, Justin Edwards was responsible for turning the early temperance movement into a full religious crusade. He disagreed with reformers who believed temperance could be achieved solely by appeals to reason. Convinced that only the fear of God would inspire the deep emotional drive that would bring success, Edwards worked to put the whole of the Protestant church behind the movement and to make the fight against liquor a gospel of Christian faith.

He soon raised enough money to pay not only his own salary but also to appoint an assistant, the Reverend Nathaniel Hewitt of Fairfield, Connecticut. They modeled their organization on the successful American Bible Society, working everywhere through the churches, seeking pledged converts. The national group would serve as a clearinghouse for other temperance movements and as a propaganda and publicity agency. Like the missionaries the churches sent to foreign lands, the American Temperance Society's mission-aries would preach to the "alcoholic savages" of America.

During their first year's crusading from church pulpits, Edwards and Hewitt revived old temperance groups, created new ones, signed hundreds of people to pledges and raised funds to hire additional agents. Within three years there were more than one thousand affiliated societies, and in another five years the number rose to more than six thousand and had spread to every state. National governing councils of the Presbyterian, Methodist, Congregational, Baptist and other Protestant churches endorsed and encouraged the work.

Temperance meetings took on the emotional fervor of religious revivals, with weeping, shouting, singing demonstrations and parades of those who testified that they had been saved. Speaker after speaker, in tones of threatening pulpit oratory, warned the drinker that he would face the searing agonies of Hell and deny himself the happiness of earthly life and the rewards of Heaven.

The temperance groups poured out reports, journals, tracts, pamphlets and almanacs in an unceasing flow. Much of the writing was highly emotional, filled with dogmatic statements, sweeping generalizations and wildly inaccurate statistics. Tales of drunkards who died of "spontaneous combustion" from a sort of "internal fire" that consumed them were widely believed. Doctors, educators and even distinguished scientists offered "proof" that a drunkard's alcoholic breath could be ignited by the pipe he smoked, and produced "case histories" of drunks who supposedly exploded in horrible bursts of self-generated fire.

Popular magazines were filled with poetry and short stories of lost love, broken marriages, poverty and terrible death that came from drinking, and children's books offered temperance parodies of well-known nursery rhymes and frightening tales of drinking fathers who let children starve to death or freeze in the winter cold. Theatrical managers cashed in on the popular interest by dramatizing drunkenness in plays, and song sheets popularized such lyrics as "The Rumseller's Lament," "Dear Father Drink No More" and "Mother Dry That Flowing Tear."

But while all the temperance groups agreed that liquor was evil, they nearly all disagreed over what should be done about it. State and local societies often worked at cross-purposes. Some shunned habitual drunkards as being beyond salvation and concentrated on getting moderate drinkers to give up liquor. Others argued that the fight should be directed against the manufacturers and sellers of liquor. There were many who were still for moderation rather than for a ban against all drinking.

In some local societies members were allowed to take pledges which permitted them to drink light wines and beer. Others who took the pledge of total abstinence from all forms of intoxicating drink had the letter "T" for "total" put after their names and were called "teetotalers," a term that came into lasting use to mean any person who completely shunned alcohol.

Edwards and the national society called upon all state and local groups throughout the country to hold mass meetings and demonstrations in February, 1832. The following year, at Independence Hall in Philadelphia, a national convention formed a new federated organization which eventually became the American Temperance Union, designed to concentrate on definite goals directed by a national leadership.

Many were convinced, by the growing number of societies and pledges, that moral persuasion soon would turn all America dry. Membership grew by leaps and bounds. Edwards addressed both houses of congress and got the use of the chamber of the House of Representatives for a temperance rally, which was enthusiastically attended by many senators and congressmen. Former President John Quincy Adams occupied the seat of honor. Temperance speeches were made by congressional leaders, and the greatest orator of the senate, Daniel Webster, presented a resolution calling upon the nation's lawmakers to band together to fight the evils of drink by moral leadership and personal example.

There was no suggestion that congress should pass laws to restrict drinking. The temperance society wasn't seeking legislation, but only the influence that statesmen might have on the citizens of the nation. An American Congressional Temperance Society was formed, and a number of lawmakers of both houses pledged themselves to abstain from the use of alcohol. Lesser politicians throughout the country quickly copied the leaders of congress and organized temperance societies among members of various state legislatures.

Temperance leaders issued glowing reports of the strength of their membership, the rapid spread of new societies, the signing of pledges. They claimed that millions of Americans had been turned from drink, that hundreds of distilleries had shut down, that thousands of taverns had been closed—all as a result of moral persuasion, religious faith and the conscience of man.

But for all their optimism, the followers of temperance remained a small minority of the total population. To a great extent those who had signed pledges were already believers in the cause or were people who lost their momentary zeal as the enthusiasm and novelty of crusades wore off.

Among the most active reformers the controversies sometimes grew bitter. There were disputes with the national leadership. Some groups quit over the queston of moderate drinking. The movement gradually lost its driving force. Other causes began to attract more active public interest, and while there was still strong sentiment against liquor, the crusading spirit slowly died.

It was revived temporarily not by the organized temperance societies or by the churches, but by a group of half a dozen self-confessed drunkards who were in the habit of spending their evenings at Chase's Tavern in Baltimore. Old friends of long standing, they included two blacksmiths, a tailor, a carpenter, a coachmaker and a silversmith. They were well into their cups on an April evening in 1840 when some of them decided, more as a joke than anything else, to go to a nearby church and hear a visiting temperance lecturer from New York, the Reverend Matthew Smith.

Those who went to the meeting were so moved by what they heard that they returned to the bar and talked the others into joining them in a real attempt to break their nightly habit of getting drunk. The six old drunkards decided then and there to form themselves into a society named after George Washington and to pledge "as gentlemen" that they would give up all intoxicating liquor. They chose tailor William Mitchell to put the pledge in writing, signed it, elected themselves as officers and declared they would hold regular meetings. Each member promised to bring a drunken friend to the next meeting, who in turn might bring another friend to the next one, so that the society for the self-help of alcoholics would grow.

Baltimore newspapers, half-jokingly at first, wrote about the Washingtonians, and the group attracted such a following that within a few weeks they had to hire a hall for their meetings. By the end of the year more than a thousand men had signed the Washingtonian pledge, and the membership continued to grow. From the start, they made it clear that the society was dedicated to the reform of drunkards by those who themselves were reformed drunkards. Religion, the

37

church and speakers of the regular temperance societies were kept out at the beginning. The only speakers at meetings were those who could tell of their personal experiences with alcohol and testify about the benefits they had gained in giving it up.

The "experience meetings" drew hundreds of listeners, who were thrilled by the often shocking public confessions of sin, crime and personal ruin, and by the joyous testimonies of redemption. Men who had considered themselves outcasts of society suddenly found themselves in the spotlight of attention, receiving praise, encouragement, the understanding of former fellow drunkards and the warm sympathy of the public. Some who had never spoken in public discovered an unsuspected talent for oratory.

Among them was John Hawkins, a hatter by trade, who told how his young daughter had helped him to see the light after he had been almost continuously drunk for fifteen years. His story was published in a booklet, *Hannah Hawkins, or, The Reformed Drunkard's Daughter,* which went through twenty editions and was widely read and quoted. Hawkins devoted his life to the cause, lectured in every state of the Union, won thousands of signatures to pledges and later noted in his journal that he had traveled some 200,000 miles to address more than five thousand different groups. In 1841 Hawkins was a member of a delegation of Washingtonians who carried their message to New York, where a series of eighteen meetings, climaxed by a great open-air rally in City Hall Park, won the pledges of nearly two thousand New Yorkers.

On the first anniversary of the forming of the group, the greatest temperance demonstration the country had yet seen was staged in Baltimore. Every temperance organization for miles around joined in a parade of six thousand delegates, each society carrying its own banners as they marched through the streets singing temperance songs. Requests for speakers came to the Washingtonians from all over the country, and the Baltimore society soon began sending out teams of reformed drunkards to spread the message, two by two, across the land. Everywhere they went, other drunkards rushed forward to confess their troubles in public before audiences often left weeping by their tragic stories.

Sixty thousand men signed pledges in Ohio, thirty thousand in Kentucky, more thousands in Pennsylvania, New Jersey, upstate New York, Maryland, Virginia, to the far West and deep South, until one newspaper commented that "the whole country is in a blaze." Hundreds of Washingtonian societies were organized in cities and small towns and set to work rounding up local alcoholics. Auxiliaries brought women actively into the temperance crusade for the first time.

The Washingtonians produced an army of speakers and a dozen newspapers that were devoted to the work. They not only attracted drunkards who wanted to swear off liquor but also convinced more moderate drinkers to abstain. More than ever before, temperance was in the news. There were mass demonstrations in every city the Washingtonians visited, parades, open-air meetings, impressive pageants of floats and cheering crowds along the streets. As brass bands played, people sang, "The teetotalers are coming!"

But the movement collapsed almost as swiftly as it had risen. Interest faded in one community after another almost as soon as the emotional revivals ended and the speakers had left for the next town. There was no national organization, no permanent membership. Each local Washingtonian society made its own rules and went its own way, and nothing held them together except the momentary zeal produced by the "experience meetings." Older temperance societies, who welcomed the Washingtonians at first, began to turn against them because of lost funds and lost prestige for their own groups, and many reformers became jealous of all the attention the newcomers were getting. Although the Washingtonians claimed the reform of a million drunkards, some of those who eagerly rushed forward to take the pledge soon returned to their old habits when they found themselves no longer the center of public excitement.

Within a few years, the Washingtonian movement was no longer important. The great surge of publicity ended, and the older organizations found membership dropping off. Temperance reformers, once so optimistic that success was near, began to admit that moral persuasion was not enough to dry up America.

5

The whole strength of the early temperance movement had been in its appeal to drinkers to decide for themselves to give up liquor. Leaders publicly declared they would never seek laws to force people to quit drinking and that their campaign was strictly educational and not political. But within ten years what had been a moral crusade turned into a political one, directed not against the habits of the individual drinker but toward a demand for the total destruction of the liquor trade through the force of law.

Moral persuasion was still used in an attempt to destroy the influence of the makers and sellers of liquor and to portray the whole industry as sinful and evil, and it had a lasting effect in giving Americans a far different attitude toward moderate drinking than that held by people in most other countries. But political activity became far more important. In state and local battles against the liquor industry, the anti-liquor crusaders developed the methods and tactics that would be followed for nearly a century by those who finally brought national prohibition to the United States.

As the temperance movement began to lose strength, and as the reformers realized that, despite all their pleas, most people went on drinking as much as before, they adopted the view that what they had failed to accomplish by appeals to reason, conscience and religious faith had to be brought about by law. If the majority of Americans refused to give up liquor, then the reformers felt that for the nation's own good the laws had to be changed to make them give it up. They began to bombard city councils, boards of aldermen and state legislatures with petitions to repeal laws that sanctioned the sale of hard liquor. By the middle 1840s, temperance lobbies were busily at work in most big cities and in nearly every state legislature.

The first state-wide attacks were aimed at putting grog-shops out of business. Massachusetts in 1838 passed a law which in effect forbade retail sales. Anybody who wanted to buy liquor had to buy at least fifteen gallons of it, "delivered and carried away all at one time." But the Massachusetts law had little effect, since there was nothing in it to compel strict enforcement, and after a political fight that went on for two years, the law was repealed. Somewhat the same thing happened in several other states.

Reformers then tried to put through local option laws to let towns or counties decide whether to issue licenses. But again victories were temporary. A town that went dry in one election would vote wet the following November. Even where drys held their gains, laws were almost impossible to enforce. Liquor was bootlegged into dry areas, and in many places retailers simply ignored the law or paid small fines and went on operating as usual.

Temperance leaders, hardly able to celebrate one small

victory before they learned of defeat somewhere else, became disillusioned and decided that full state-wide prohibition was needed. In 1847 a decision by the United States Supreme Court reinforced their determination to dry up the nation state by state.

Daniel Webster was hired by a group of liquor dealers to carry an appeal to the Supreme Court in the hope that it would declare state laws regulating liquor sales unconstitutional. Three suits involving license laws in Massachusetts, Rhode Island and New Hampshire were grouped together, and the battle went on before the court for nearly two years. Webster argued that state liquor laws were unconstitutional because congress had granted foreign nations commercial treaties that authorized the import and sale of liquor and the states were bound to receive and permit the sale of any article of import authorized by congress. The states, he claimed, were interfering with the powers of the federal government.

But when the Supreme Court finally handed down its decision in 1847, it unanimously held that the states not only had full power to regulate liquor sales but also to entirely prohibit intoxicating liquors. "Every state . . . may regulate its own internal traffic, according to its own judgment, and upon its own views of the interest and well-being of its citizens," Chief Justice Roger Taney wrote in his opinion. "If any state deems the retail and internal traffic in ardent spirits injurious to its citizens, and calculated to produce idleness, vice and debauchery, I see nothing in the Constitution of the United States to prevent it from regulating and restraining the traffic, or from prohibiting it altogether, if it thinks proper."

Across the country, temperance groups held public meetings of rejoicing. Lobbyists went to work in nearly every state capital to try to put through prohibition laws without delay. But while the court had held that such laws could be adopted, getting them passed was another matter. Attention centered on Maine, where a struggle for prohibition had been under way for ten years.

It was started by James Appleton, a retired Army general with time and money to indulge in all sorts of social reforms. In 1837, as chairman of a joint legislative committee appointed to study the problem, Appleton submitted a report that called for repeal of liquor licensing and recommended a law to prohibit all traffic of any kind in liquor anywhere in the state. It was the first time in the nation's history that a legislative committee had called for complete prohibition, and Appleton was credited with being America's first real prohibitionist. No action was taken, and Maine's lawmakers quickly tabled the report without debate. But it inspired another reformer, Neal Dow, to take command of the battle Appleton had started.

Born in 1804 into a Quaker household where alcohol was strictly forbidden, Dow was hardly out of knee-pants before he began advocating temperance. As a youth, he persuaded the Portland volunteer fire company to adopt a no-drink rule, succeeded in having liquor banned at Fourth of July celebrations and talked a state association of master mechanics into going on record against liquor rations for helpers and apprentices. Dow built the family's leather-tanning business into an important industry, became a successful speculator in timber lands and a prosperous investor in other businesses and used all his increasing influence to fight drinking, which he considered not only a moral evil but one which offended his Yankee sense of thrift.

When the Maine Temperance Society refused to call for a pledge against the drinking of beer and wine as well as rum and whiskey, Dow resigned, took his friends with him and formed his own rival Maine Temperance Union into a political action group. Declaring that Maine would never be free of intemperance until the manufacture and sale of liquor was made a prison offense, he began a political war to dry up every drinking place in the state.

In 1842, as a result of Dow's door-to-door crusading, Portland became the first major city to ban the legal retail sale of intoxicants by a direct vote of the people. But the action backfired because most of the city's drinking places simply became speakeasies, and without licensing control almost anybody who felt like it opened a bar. Dozens of illegal establishments sprang up. Liquor flowed freely into Portland from the rest of the state, and police and the courts showed no particular desire to interfere. Seeing victory turn to defeat, Dow became even more convinced that state-wide prohibition was the only answer.

He then began a battle that was to go on for nearly ten years, first to bring prohibition to Maine and then to strengthen and enforce it. In the process he became the state's political boss, and Maine became the first testing grounds of the methods that later generations of temperance reformers would use. Dow urged Maine's prohibitionists to ignore established political parties and to get out and campaign actively, district by district, to elect members of the legislature who would promise to adopt prohibition regardless of which political party they represented. Party lines had to be crossed, he argued, political differences had to be put aside, and all other issues had to be made secondary.

By 1844 he had enough political strength to get a legislative committee to introduce a prohibition bill and to get it through the lower house, but it failed in the state senate. Dow considered that only the first skirmish. While lobbyists kept up their pressure in the state capital, he organized teams of workers to visit every community and took the lead himself in arousing public opinion. To bring out large audiences for meetings, he provided singers, musicians and other enter-

45

tainers. He traveled through storms and over snow-drifted roads, and in the two months just before the next election personally covered four thousand miles, crisscrossing back and forth over the state to appeal to thousands of voters.

He was able to muster a majority in both houses of the legislature by the time the 1846 session met. A prohibition bill was introduced and quickly passed, but it put enforcement in the hands of local authorities rather than the state, and there were so many loopholes for evasion that the law was totally ineffective. Dow pressured the legislature into passing an amendment to appoint special officers in each town "to ferret out and suppress the grogshops," but Governor John Dana vetoed the measure and attacked the whole idea of prohibition, declaring there was no way of ever enforcing it anywhere.

Dow was determined to prove it could be enforced and chose his own city of Portland as a test. In 1850, in a contest that split the city's regular political parties wide open, he was elected mayor. In the same election, his forces won firm control of both houses of the state legislature, put Governor Dana out of office and elected their own man, country doctor John Hubbard, as governor.

With that kind of political power behind him, Dow dictated the membership of a special legislative committee to draft the exact prohibition law he wanted. Within ten days, he had it put before the legislature and directed the lobby that kept it from being amended. Wets waged a delaying last-ditch fight, but the legislature overwhelmingly approved it and on June 2, 1851, Governor Hubbard signed Dow's law.

It forbade all manufacture and sale of intoxicating liquors in the state, and provided for tight enforcement and for search and seizure warrants to be issued on the complaint of as few as three voters. To put local officers eagerly behind enforcement, the law let them keep any fines collected by the courts.

Mayor Dow set an enforcement example in Portland by ordering liquor merchants and barkeepers to get rid of every drop they had within a matter of days. When the deadline passed, Dow personally led his raiders into tippling shops, with his own hands smashed barrels and kegs and publicly poured thousands of dollars' worth of rum and whiskey into the gutter in front of City Hall. Within months, he claimed his city was bone-dry and began issuing enthusiastic reports on the success of the Maine law to temperance groups around the country.

The victory in Maine gave brief new life to the whole temperance movement. A National Temperance Convention, meeting in Saratoga Springs, New York, recommended the Maine law "to all friends of temperance to cherish as the sure and the only triumph of their cause, and continually to urge its adoption upon every legislature." In the first wave of prohibition, laws similar to Maine's were passed within the next four years by twelve states, from New England to the Midwest. In half a dozen others, battles were narrowly lost. New Hampshire in 1855 passed a stringent version of the Maine law.

But that was the last of the string of victories, and it was almost a quarter of a century before another state adopted prohibition. Temperance leaders, at first jubilantly confident that within a short time the whole United States, state by state, would choose prohibition, saw their gains slowly melt away. In some states, the laws were ruled unconstitutional, and in others the voters rebelled and demanded the return of liquor. One by one, every state that had voted prohibition either repealed or drastically modified its law, until Maine itself was the only one where full prohibition remained in force.

There were many reasons. In some places laws had been put through almost before people realized what was happening. Other hastily enacted laws failed to work, and voters became disgusted with the tangle of enforcement problems. Liquor interests recovered from their first defeats and began to match the pressure groups of the reformers. But more than anything else, what really halted the first prohibition movement was the growing threat of Civil War.

Embroiled in the troubles that were tearing the nation itself apart, most Americans lost interest in less crucial issues. Many temperance leaders were abolitionists, and as they turned to fighting slavery they had little time for other causes. To the average person, concerned with the threat of a terrible civil war, it hardly seemed important to argue over whether a man should take a drink. When war did come, prohibition was all but forgotten as both the North and South struggled with more immediate life-and-death problems.

The Civil War delivered a still more staggering blow to the cause of prohibition when the federal government adopted the Internal Revenue Act as an emergency measure to raise the money that was desperately needed to prosecute the war. Hotly debated in congress, it was passed July 1, 1862, and imposed a federal fee on every retail liquor establishment in the Union, as well as a direct federal tax by the gallon on the manufacture of liquor, beer and ale. Opponents charged that it amounted to federal licensing of the liquor trade.

President Lincoln signed the Internal Revenue Act with the implied promise that the liquor tax would be repealed as soon as the Civil War was over. But, like most tax measures, it remained on the books and grew to be the single most important source of funds for financing the entire national government in the years before there were direct income and profits taxes. From 1870 to 1915 the liquor tax provided between one-half and two-thirds of the whole internal revenue of the United States.

After it was adopted, the drys had to fight not only the fact that the liquor industry had the stamp of federal approval, but also that many people in government favored and encouraged increased sales of liquor to produce more federal funds. The liquor tax was providing some two hundred million dollars a year after the turn of the century, and through the years one of the strongest arguments against prohibition was that it would greatly increase all other taxes by cutting off a good part of the money that came in to run the government.

Suffering successive attacks from all sides after their first quick victories, the prohibitionists found little to encourage them through the 1860s. But a new force was rising in the temperance movement—the power of women, who were beginning to demand the right to speak out on such issues. Their determination to battle the demon rum became an emotional fury that threw much of the United States into an uproar.

6

The Woman's Crusade of the 1870s, which sent bands of singing, praying, emotionally aroused women swarming into the saloons of twenty states to shut them down like a "whirlwind of the Lord," began with a man. He was Dr. Dioclesian Lewis, a smooth-talking spellbinder, regarded by some as hardly more than a charlatan, but by others as an outstanding health expert, educator, writer and advanced thinker. Sometimes called the founder of physical education in the United States, Lewis was credited among other things with inventing the wooden dumbbell and the bean-bag for indoor exercise.

Lewis apparently gave himself the title of "Doctor" after studying for two years at Harvard, and he established schools and sanatoriums, hotels and public resorts dedicated to his ideals of physical fitness. He was also a pioneer of dental hygiene. He founded and edited newspapers and magazines to promote his theories and was a prolific author of health books that became best-sellers.

Along with his writing and running schools and health resorts, Lewis' greatest success was as a public speaker. He was a highly paid star of the lyceum circuit who spoke each year in dozens of cities across the United States, and was especially adored by female audiences. Well along in years when he inspired the Woman's Crusade of the 1870s, Lewis still was described as a handsome, blue-eyed six-footer, with flowing white hair and a "peachy complexion" that made him a vigorous example of his own health teachings.

Early in December, 1873, after a regular lyceum appearance the day before, Lewis gave a Sunday evening temperance talk at the Baptist church in Fredonia, New York. He told a story of his youth forty years before in the village of Clarksville, about how churchwomen banded together and marched upon the saloons and, by singing hymns and praying, drove the barkeepers out of business. The story inspired his listeners in Fredonia. The Baptist women stayed after his talk, organized a committee to try the same thing, and marched out to sing hymns in Fredonia's saloons.

Their mission accomplished little, but Lewis realized he had hit upon a popular theme. He went on to make several speeches in nearby Pennsylvania, expanding on the idea that the women of America could conquer the liquor traffic with "faith and prayer" by applying the "Christian principle of love" through "visitation bands." But it wasn't until Lewis reached Ohio that his idea really caught on.

Two nights before Christmas, 1873, he brought his message to the little town of Hillsboro, Ohio, a "quiet, cultured and refined" community of three thousand people and the home of two colleges for young women. It was also a place with thirteen saloons and a drugstore that sold liquor. Lewis had been scheduled to give a "literary lecture," as part of the regular lyceum program, but he devoted his talk instead to temperance and repeated his by then well-rehearsed story of the female uprising against the saloons when he was a boy, exhorting the women of Hillsboro to follow that example.

"The Doctor spoke with enthusiasm, and seeing him so full of faith, the hearts of the women seized the hope—a forlorn one 'tis true, but still a hope," said the 800-page *History of the Woman's Temperance Crusade*, written by Annie Wittenmyer, later the first president of the Woman's Christian Temperance Union. "When Dr. Lewis asked if they were willing to undertake the task, scores of women rose to their feet. . . . A strange work was to be done, and by unaccustomed hands."

A meeting was called for the following morning at the Presbyterian church by a committee that named Hillsboro's most prominent woman, Mrs. Eliza J. Thompson, daughter of a former governor, to head it. A gentle and retiring woman in her sixties, deeply religious and known for her charitable works, she had been unable to attend Lewis' lecture, and had no knowledge that the others had chosen her until her son came home and told her, "Ma, they've got you into business."

Her husband, who had been taking a nap, raised himself on one elbow and commented that the whole thing sounded to him like a lot of "tomfoolery." Nettled, Mrs. Thompson, according to her own story, told him, "Well, husband, the men have been in the tomfoolery business a long time. Perhaps the Lord is going to call us into partnership with them." Thompson turned to his son, pointed to the Bible and said, "We all know where your mother will take this case for counsel."

Mrs. Thompson, who had never taken part in any kind of a protest and who confessed to a horror of making herself conspicuous in public, went to a corner of the room, knelt before the opened Bible and in the 146th Psalm found the words ". . . but the way of the wicked he turneth upside down." She had wanted to "see what God would say to me" and she "knew that was for me" and when she went to the church the next morning "a hundred ladies were assembled . . . and before I could get to the pulpit, they had put me in office—I was their leader."

For her work in the crusade, she was to become nationally known as "Mother Thompson." As she later wrote, "Many of our men were there, and our ministers also. They stayed a few minutes and then rose and went out, saying, 'This is your work—we leave it with the women and the Lord.' When they had gone, I just opened the big pulpit Bible and read the 146th Psalm and told them the circumstance of my selecting it. The women sobbed so I could hardly go on." She led them in prayer and then said, "Now, ladies, let us file out, two by two, the smallest first, and let us sing as we go."

The old hymn "Give to the Winds Thy Fears" was chosen. Some singing, some praying, some weeping, all transported by religious exaltation, the women marched out of the church and down the main street to the nearest saloon. They pushed their way inside, ignored the protest of the startled saloonkeeper that "it's a sin and a shame to pray in a saloon" and knelt on the sawdust floor in prayer. There they meant to come and to stay, they told him, until he signed the pledge and destroyed his stock of liquor and went out of business. And so began a remarkable and hysterical demonstration that was to sweep from village to village until much of the nation and a good part of the world was aroused by the stories told of it.

For two months, with special prayer meetings each morning and mass meetings each evening, the women kept up their marching, praying and hymn-singing assaults on the drinking places of Hillsboro, day after day, until the bars in all but one hotel and two saloons were closed. Some of the drinking places went bankrupt for lack of business. Others gave in to the aroused feelings of the town. One saloonkeeper, driven finally to a nervous collapse by the constant hounding, threw himself face-down on the floor and sobbingly prayed for peace before agreeing to quit the business and open a fish store.

Meanwhile, Dioclesian Lewis had moved on into neighboring towns to touch off similar demonstrations, each encouraged by the reported successes in other places. He gave up his regular lyceum tour to devote himself entirely to the Woman's Crusade, and women from the places where the movement had already caught fire appeared with him to encourage others to take up what they considered "God's call" to carry out "a sacred mission." They told many stories of "Heavenly intervention" and their accounts were filled with "testimony" of supernatural happenings: saloonkeepers reportedly turned mute or struck dead, drinking places consumed by mysterious fires, ferocious dogs that "scented a Presence" and turned away. Many women believed they were not only inspired but were the chosen instruments of the Lord.

Scores and then tens of thousands of women joined the "praying bands" as the excitement flamed from Ohio through some three hundred towns and cities, into Indiana, Illinois, West Virginia, Pennsylvania, New York, Michigan, Wisconsin, Iowa, Missouri, California and Oregon. There were many demonstrations in Eastern states and in New England, but the uproar centered in the Midwest and was more successful in small towns and rural areas than in large cities.

At first, most saloonkeepers treated the demonstrations as a joke. Customers watched with amusement as the ladies knelt on the barroom floors to pray. But the saloonkeepers soon began to lock their doors to keep the praying women out. The ladies then gathered on the walks and knelt in the streets outside, ringed by crowds of curious townspeople. They kept up their street vigils through freezing weather, rain and snow, until public opinion was aroused to back them and demand the closing of the saloons. Church bells rang every hour, public meetings were told of each day's triumphs and big-city newspapers began to send correspondents and artists to dramatically depict the happenings. Women who never before had dared risk public attention found themselves lifted from small-town obscurity to the front pages.

Bands of men tried to hoot them down, and to taunt them with ribald jokes and often obscene remarks. Some women were arrested and jailed for interfering with licensed businesses. Others were pummeled, pushed around and molested, or had their clothing torn. In some towns special bands of police, armed with clubs, drove them from the streets, only to see them come marching back in greater numbers. Women were locked up and held prisoner in some saloons they entered; were threatened with knives, guns and even old Civil War cannon; or were frightened by displays of blood-smeared axes and the stringing up of skull-and-crossbones flags. Men dragged life-sized straw-stuffed dummies representing the Crusade's leaders through the streets and staged mock hangings. Some saloonkeepers hired brass bands in attempts to drown out the hymn singing, paid boys to dance around the kneeling women and toot on tin horns or soaked them with water hoses, pails of beer and slops. In places there was open rioting.

But the women, for the most part calmly, came day upon day, quietly pleading with the sellers of liquor to seek "God's love and forgiveness." Brewers and distillers backed the saloonkeepers, often supplying them with free liquor, paying court costs and providing attorneys. Some of the saloonkeepers set up portable taverns and wagons that went around doling out free beer, and the women countered by setting up portable street tabernacles for prayer.

The Woman's Crusade was at its height for only six months. Started in the winter of 1873, it was already beginning to die out by the following summer. But while it lasted, several thousand drinking places were closed. Even the federal government felt the effect in the heavy loss of liquor taxes. The Crusade had done nothing, however, to change the laws, and the closing of the saloons was only temporary. Within a year nearly every town where the women had crusaded had as many drinking places as before.

But it drew out of their sheltered homes women who had hardly dared think for themselves, broke down social and church barriers that had surrounded them, brought them into contact with others of different classes and took them into the streets to see conditions to which they had blinded themselves. Though many of its followers shied away from any radical talk of "woman's rights," the Crusade became an emotional outburst against the restrictions that had held women down. Fundamentally it was a female revolution against the old stay-at-home traditions imposed upon women by men.

The world-wide publicity gained by the Crusaders gave new enthusiasm to the whole temperance movement and made the country more temperance-minded. Old temperance groups were revived, new political action groups were formed and both congress and state legislatures gradually became more receptive to appeals for anti-liquor legislation. A more direct result was the start of what was to become for many years the largest women's organization of any kind in the world.

While the Crusade was still going strong, women in a

number of communities began to establish local and state temperance unions. During the summer of 1874 many of the leaders met at a Sunday school conference at Chautauqua, New York. They talked over the need for a permanent organization and issued a call for a convention in Cleveland. Two hundred women from seventeen states met there in November, 1874, organized what they called the Woman's National Christian Temperance Union, adopted a constitution and invited the state groups to affiliate "to preserve the fruits of the Crusade." The W.C.T.U. soon declared that "we hold prohibition to be essential to the full triumph of this reform," a position it never abandoned.

Its early strength was built almost entirely by Frances Willard, a witty, intelligent and seldom grim reformer, who saw in the Union a chance to help women free themselves from the domination of men, as well as from the tragedies liquor brought to many homes. Something of a radical, she was a latecomer to the temperance movement, and in its cause became one of the most prominent women her century produced.

When the Crusade swept across the Midwest, Frances Elizabeth Willard was a middle-aged woman who had become an outstanding educator and a speaker for woman's rights. Although she had been surrounded from childhood by those who thought liquor was evil, she had never taken an active part in the organized temperance movement.

Born in Churchville, New York, on September 28, 1839, she was taken to the Midwest by her parents, who moved as covered wagon pioneers to an isolated farm near Janesville, Wisconsin, and later to Evanston, Illinois. She grew up with a brother and sister, shut off almost entirely from outside companionship, her life ruled by the harsh discipline of her overly religious father, who dominated the household. Chilled and alienated by her father's narrow views, she rebelliously grew into a tomboy, was nine years old before she could write her own name and didn't begin her formal schooling until she was fifteen.

After attending a newly established college for young ladies at Evanston, where she was greatly influenced by the writings of Margaret Fuller and other pioneer feminists, she became a country school teacher at about the time the Civil War started. In seven years, Frances Willard worked her way up from teaching in a one-room schoolhouse to the faculty of several women's colleges, and in 1872 became Dean of Women at Northwestern University.

She had traveled over much of the United States, spent a year touring Europe from Ireland to Russia, innovated many teaching methods and was beginning to gain prominence as an educator, writer and speaker. But she had a battle with the male faculty of Northwestern, charged that the men were robbing her of all authority to put her educational ideas into practice and resigned.

In June, 1874, when she quit as Northwestern's Dean of Women, excitement over the Woman's Crusade was at its peak and she was stirred by the uprising of women to accomplish a reform in which men had failed. Although liquor had always been banned in her family's home and in the homes of most of her friends, she knew little about the temperance movement. So she packed her bags and traveled East to discuss it directly with two of its leaders, Neal Dow of Maine and the convincing Doctor Dioclesian Lewis. From them and others, she heard enough to become fully convinced that the male world of saloons helped enforce the unfair domination of women and stood in the way of their attempts to create better communities, to have a voice in public affairs and to seek education and equality.

She was offered a chance to become principal of a fashionable school for girls in New York City at a high salary, and Wellesley College also invited her to join its faculty; but she turned down those and other offers. She had made up her mind that there was more opportunity for leadership in the revived temperance movement. When a group of Chicago women asked her to head their organization, she accepted even though the pay was small. She went to Chautauqua, New York, where the formation of a national woman's temperance union was being discussed, and became acquainted with its leaders.

On her way home to Illinois she stopped in Pittsburgh to visit a friend who was a public school teacher and to take part with her in one of the last of the marching crusades against the saloons. "Two school-ma'ms together, we fell into the procession behind the experienced crusaders," she wrote. Driven from a saloon by the "bacchanalian curses" of brawling men, the women knelt outside at the curbstone in prayer. "With a heart stirred as never until now by human sin and shame, I joined in the sweet gospel song," she wrote. "Just such an epoch as that was in my life, has the Crusade proved to a mighty army of women all over this land. . . . Need I say it was the Crusade that opened before me, as before ten thousand other women, this wide effectual door?"

At a meeting in Bloomington, Illinois, she was chosen secretary of the state women's temperance group and was named a delegate to the national organizing convention in Cleveland. There, in September, 1874, Frances Willard was elected corresponding secretary of the national Woman's Christian Temperance Union. It was a key position that put her in charge of linking the activities of all the state and local groups with the national organization, and from the start, Frances Willard became the driving personality behind its growth.

The W.C.T.U. was first led by wealthy and conservative women who hoped to make it an extension of church and missionary work in reforming the character and conduct of the lower classes. The conservatives wanted to hold the W.C.T.U. to the single cause of temperance. But Frances Willard had far more liberal views. She fought to link it with every reform that would change social, political and economic conditions that led to intemperance. Instead of simply waging a missionary crusade against individual drinking habits, she advocated a "do everything" policy that would make the W.C.T.U. an agency of change rather than a group dedicated to preserving the status quo. She wanted it identified by the public with progressive forces, and she saw the winning of public opinion as its main role and education as the key to it.

She gradually won control, and after she was elected national president in 1879 she molded the organization to her views. Sometimes they were too radical to win the support of the entire membership, but for the next nineteen years, until her death in 1898, she firmly held the leadership of what became the first great national organization of women.

By establishing and energetically directing some fifty different departments of the W.T.C.U., all actively at work across the nation in all sorts of reforms linked with temperance, she encouraged women of all classes, ages and interests to join. There were groups dedicated to improved home cooking, gardening and better nutrition, family health, physical exercise for women and welfare work, and others to promote school education in alcoholism, political action, economic research, legislation and contacts with labor and indutry. The W.C.T.U. offered something for every woman, housewife or intellectual, conservative or progressive. It grew from a few thousand members in scattered groups to a tightly knit national force with branches in nearly every town and city in the United States, and eventually in many foreign lands.

Frances Willard turned its power, and her own as a commanding writer and eloquent speaker, to the support of woman's suffrage and the organized labor movement, against the crushing economic greed of employers who kept workers in conditions of poverty, and against political, business and social institutions that stood in the way not only of prohibition but of other reforms. She worked for a better civil service system, improved laws applying to the Indians and greater freedom in women's fashions and with a sense of humor battled even minor customs that restricted women. Daringly, at a time when men were shocked by such actions, she not only rode a bicycle in public, but then wrote a book about it, *A Wheel Within a Wheel, or How to Ride a Bicycle.*

With her close personal friend Terrence Powderly, leader of the Knights of Labor, a pioneer union organization of half a million men, she often joined forces in crusades not only to promote the aims of the W.C.T.U. but to put it behind demands for better working conditions, higher pay, a shorter work week and more stable employment. At a period when collective bargaining was unknown, she urged such dealings between management and labor through conciliation "as opposed to greed in gain." She put the W.C.T.U. on record with a declaration that "we believe in a living wage; in an eight-hour day."

She argued that while liquor caused poverty, the reverse also was true and that poor wages and living conditions drove men to drink. Personally her left-wing political leanings were toward a form of socialism that favored the working classes rather than big business, financial trusts and political advantage for the wealthy. Calling herself a "collectivist," she said she believed the fruits and burdens of society "should be distributed according to those principles of justice which ought to teach every human being that every other has as much right as himself to life, liberty and the pursuit of happiness."

Because the major political parties avoided taking a stand on the prohibition question, Frances Willard helped organize various minor political parties that would support it. She put the endorsement of the W.C.T.U. behind them. But when they failed to win any great following of voters, she came to the conclusion that public opinion had to be strengthened before any real political victory could be won. Under her direction, the W.C.T.U. and all its agencies and activities became a vast organ of propaganda. Booklets, pamphlets and other printed material, a newspaper information service, articles, speeches and work in every branch across the country prepared the ground for the coming of national prohibition.

The W.C.T.U.'s greatest success was in promoting its views among young people, the voters of the future, through temperance teaching in the public schools. The women went to work to organize political strength in the various legislatures, and with lobbies, pressure groups and petitions, they gradually won the passage of laws that made "scientific" study of temperance compulsory in the schools.

Eventually the study of the effects of drinking alcohol was required by law in forty states and territories. In some states influence was so strong that school authorities invited the selection and editing of textbooks to conform to W.C.T.U. policy. Most of the texts carefully avoided an outright demand for prohibition, but the idea was firmly planted through classroom readings, recitations and "natural science experiments" that liquor was a personal and national poison.

By the time Frances Willard died in 1898, she was a

living legend. States would declare her birthday a school holiday, hospitals, schools and public buildings would be named after her, congress would hold memorial services, and she would be the first woman ever honored by having her statue in the nation's capital, as well as later in the Hall of Fame. But with her passing, the W.C.T.U. turned more conservative again, dropping the other reforms and causes for which she had fought and devoting itself almost entirely to the crusade against liquor.

Meanwhile, the temperance revival which grew out of the Woman's Crusade had brought the first real demands for national prohibition. Until then state prohibition had been the goal, but while battles were going on in the state legislatures many leaders began to call for federal action. Some felt that the established political parties were afraid to take a position on the question, and new political parties began to form.

In September, 1869, five hundred delegates met in Chicago to organize the Prohibition Party, which became the first national political group to demand an amendment to the Constitution. It went on for more than fifty years, nominating national, state and local candidates and campaigning for a Constitutional amendment, and although it never was more than a minor political party it exerted an influence out of proportion to the number of votes it gained. It kept prohibition alive as a political issue, forced other politicians to take notice of the question, gained much publicity and helped convert many Americans to the idea even though they cast their ballots for other candidates.

The first prohibition amendment to reach congress was introduced in the House in December, 1876, by Representative Henry W. Blair of New Hampshire. It didn't include wine or beer, but even so it was buried in committee. Four years later, a stronger amendment was proposed, but it also was bottled up and never reached the House floor. Blair, meanwhile, had been elected to the Senate, and in 1877 he offered a measure prepared with the help of Frances Willard and other officers of the W.C.T.U., as well as the National Prohibition Party and the National Temperance Society. They brought enough pressure to force it out of committee, but the Senate finally rejected it two years later by a vote of thirty-three to thirteen. It was twenty-five years before another prohibition amendment went to congress.

In the states there was great confusion over liquor laws, with all kinds of regulations being passed or repealed from year to year according to the way the political winds blew. Temperance leaders decided to work for more permanent state prohibition and began campaigning to make it part of the various state constitutions. The process was long and difficult and met with all kinds of political maneuvers and delays.

In 1881, Kansas became the first state to adopt constitutional prohibition. Maine and Rhode Island voted for constitutional prohibition, and there were temporary gains in some other states. But the drys then had a long series of setbacks. The temperance forces lacked funds and were divided by debates over whether to concentrate on state battles or put all their strength behind national prohibition. Both the Republican and Democratic political machines worked against them in the states, and whatever party was in power generally led the opposition.

Waves of immigration, meanwhile, had brought hundreds of thousands of Germans and other Europeans to settle in America, people who by long tradition tolerantly accepted the moderate drinking of beer and wine. Within the United States itself there was a migration of people from small towns and rural areas to the cities, which swelled city populations and took workers from farms into factories. The new industrial and city society was strange and frightening to many in a nation that had been largely agricultural. Saloons and the political corruption they brought were looked upon by some as an evil that grew out of the other changes that threatened the old small-town ways of life and the established social order. Prohibition grew into a battle of rural against city patterns, of native-born Americans against immigrants, of home government against political machines, of conservatives against liberals and of religious prejudice that turned many Protestants against Catholics.

Liquor interests became more organized. The United States Brewers' Association was formed, and it established a powerful and successful lobby in Washington to influence congress. Other liquor trade groups came into being. Temperance reformers were outraged to discover that liquor interests were using the same tactics and methods the drys themselves had used to capture public opinion, and in most areas the brewers and distillers had much more money to spend than the reformers.

Out of the confusion of Temperance forces, a new movement grew. Started by Dr. Howard Russell, a Protestant clergyman in Ohio, it developed into the Anti-Saloon League, with rapidly expanding branches in nearly every state. Established on a national basis in 1896, with the "suppression of the saloon" as its object, the League was a self-declared "public-sentiment building society," dedicated to "keeping the public demand on the question at a pitch of effectiveness."

The League soon took full charge of the drive for prohibition and unified the crusade, raised funds and intensified religious and emotional appeals. It became one of the most successful propaganda and political machines the nation had ever known and finally was the central force that made prohibition part of the Constitution of the United States.

7

The Anti-Saloon League, working through the churches, formed a mighty political organization that translated its strength into direct action to dry up America step by step. It worked for anti-liquor laws first in towns and villages, then in counties, then in states and finally nationwide.

Calling itself "the Church in Action against the Saloon," it raised and spent some thirty-five million dollars for propaganda and lobbying, established a printing plant that turned out nearly two tons of literature a month and tried to enlist every churchgoer in the country in direct political battle to obtain whatever advantage could be gained at any particular time or place. In addition to a small army of full-time organizers and agents, the League managed to put as many as fifty thousand volunteer speakers behind its various campaigns.

It took the League almost ten years to become firmly

established on a national basis. Agents went from church to church across the country, speaking to congregations and getting thousands of pledges of support and promises of regular contributions of from twenty-five cents to two dollars a month. Larger funds came from church organizations and wealthy laymen. Strong branches were formed in every state. The League had the active help of the national leaders of most Protestant denominations and worked out methods of cooperation with nearly all other temperance groups. Its power grew until it controlled state legislatures, dictated the choice of political candidates and eventually won a prohibition majority in congress.

Under the leadership of the Reverend Purley A. Baker of Ohio, who became national superintendent in 1903, the League operated on a level of hardheaded political realism that often was brilliant in its strategy. Working through all the established political parties, without giving blanket endorsement to any, it shrewdly played one faction off against another to gain the greatest possible influence over all politicians.

Whether a man running for office happened to be a Republican or Democrat, or whatever his other qualifications might be, made no difference to the League, as long as he was the candidate who promised the drys the best advantage in that particular election contest. Churchgoers were asked to forget party affiliations and all other issues and to unite to win political strength, little by little, regardless of where it came from. Gradually the League managed to elect many of its chosen men, to drive from office many others who opposed it and to intimidate politicians whose support for anti-liquor laws could be gained only by "teaching them a lesson" at the polls.

"The Anti-Saloon League is not a mob of long-haired fanatics," a trade magazine, *Bonfort's Wine and Spirit Cir-*

cular, warned liquor dealers as early as 1907. "It is a strongly centralized organization, officered with men of unusual ability, financiered by capitalists with long purses, subscribed to by hundreds of thousands of men, women and children who are solicited by their various churches, advised by well-paid attorneys of great ability, and it is working with definite ideas to guide it in every state, in every county, in every city, in every precinct."

When they entered an election battle, the League's agents would swarm into the area to bring every imaginable pressure to bear on candidates and officeholders. It would be saturated with literature, honeycombed with speakers and organized church by church and street by street. Quick to take full advantage of the needs of the moment, they shifted tactics, policies and alliances according to local conditions. Some agents later boasted of false rumors they spread, of tricks they played, of lies they told and even of votes they bought to outwit those they considered too evil to be dealt with honestly. Convinced they were doing "Godly work" and that the end justified the means, many took the attitude that all was fair in any battle to "beat the Devil at his own game."

But for all its success at political maneuvering, the League's real strength came from the solid backing of the growing number of Americans who agreed that the saloon and its evils should be banished. National prohibition was not the League's goal at the start. That came later, after political power had been won. The saloon was the real enemy, and the League's greatest victory was in the war of propaganda that made the very word "saloon" such a synonym for social and moral wrong that for years after the end of prohibition the term was never used to refer to any reputable drinking establishment. The drys made it a horrid word, one to which respectable people reacted emotionally, and the saloon became to many "the Devil's headquarters on earth."

The League's own printing plant at Westerville, Ohio, turned out millions of books, charts, leaflets, tracts, folders and pamphlets. It published a daily paper, a weekly journal and half a dozen other periodicals, and it prepared speeches, sermons for delivery in thousands of churches, canned editorials for newspapers and articles for magazines. Its endless flood of printed material was doubled by the output of various other temperance, church and reform groups. Year after year, people in every part of the country were bombarded with an unceasing attack which had the saloon as its main target.

The saloons most people saw in their own towns helped convince them. There were, of course, well-run establishments that stayed within the law and were friendly gathering places of good fellowship. But many of the old-time saloons fully earned the worst that could be said of them. They were dingy, dirty and disorderly. Beer, rather than hard liquor, produced the greatest profits, and brewers greedily tried to saturate communities with far more saloons than were needed. They bribed police, politicians and officials, arrogantly ignored protests and broke or evaded most laws and regulations that might interfere with the free flow of beer.

Village saloons often were no more than shacks and frequently were the places where most of the town's troubles began. Some city neighborhoods had a saloon in every block, with drunks lurching from doorways, loafers at the curbs, foul-smelling slops spilled over the sidewalks and outbursts of cursing or brawling exploding from behind the swinging doors. Corrupt political organizations centered in the saloons, organized vice spread from them and crime bred in them. They clustered around factories to get first crack at the laborer's pay, encouraged drunkenness and generally became both an abomination and an eyesore.

The propaganda battle was far from one-sided. With a billion-dollar industry at stake, the brewers and distillers waged their own war against the drys, financed by assessing the saloons. But their efforts often were politically inept and, instead of winning public opinion, backfired against them. They underestimated the strength of the opposition, laughed at the drys and mocked them instead of taking them seriously and failed to clean up the worst of the saloon conditions in a way that might have satisfied most people.

Liquor interests bought control of some big-city newspapers, financed others and put editors and well-known writers on their payroll. They lined the pockets of political leaders with money, kept the coffers of Republican and Democratic machines well filled and delivered blocs of city votes in exchange for political favors. Dummy chambers of commerce were set up, with the hidden purpose of fighting liquor laws, and at the height of the battle the wets were turning out books, pamphlets and magazines in a volume that almost matched the output of the drys.

But much of the wet propaganda was so obviously in the interest of preserving the profits of brewers and distillers that it was ineffective. There was also a bickering lack of unity among the liquor interests. Most brewers refused to believe that the saloon wouldn't go on as it was forever, but many distillers felt that the lack of any attempt to clean up the saloons was dragging the whole industry to ruin.

The Anti-Saloon League, despite the political tricks it indulged in itself, managed to make the activities of the liquor organizations seem far more scandalous. Sensational exposures of bribery, payoffs, purchased influence, blacklists and coercion served as grist for its propaganda mill, and the sordid details spread before the public shocked and disgusted respectable Americans. Many who had never strongly favored temperance came to feel in all honesty that progress, science and reform demanded an end to the saloon.

Some took up the fight less against alcohol than in the

hope of wiping out poverty, crime and corrupt political machines. The saloon became the stumbling block of all wet arguments, and around it the drys gradually built a demand for total prohibition rather than mere temperance. The fight was kept in the headlines by a star-studded cast of personal crusaders whose colorful antics captured the public interest and dramatized the battle. They included golden-voiced William Jennings Bryan, acrobatic evangelist Billy Sunday, hatchet-wielding Carry Nation and a gun-toting hero of the Wild West, Pussyfoot Johnson.

William Jennings Bryan, who had a following of millions of Americans as a three-time Democratic candidate for president, helped to turn public opinion to the drys, especially in the Midwest and South. Adored by small-town America as The Great Commoner, who battled for the farmers and the old-fashioned virtues of rural life against big cities, big business and big money interests, Bryan attacked the brewers and saloon-bred political corruption from the lecture platforms of hundreds of tents and halls as a star of the Chautauqua circuit.

Born in 1860 in Salem, Illinois, into a home where liquor was totally forbidden, he signed the pledge as soon as he was old enough to write his name and most of his life tried to convert others to give up drinking, including reporters who traveled with him on his presidential campaigns. As a student in Illinois College, he championed debating teams in the cause of temperance, even arguing that drink was more destructive than war.

After Bryan moved to Nebraska at the age of twenty-seven, to practice law and begin his career in politics, he became for a time less outspoken on the liquor question. Growing to power in the Democratic party, which welcomed the money and votes brewers could supply, he kept his personal beliefs mainly to himself. But he soon turned again to denounce the saloons, even at the risk of splitting party forces. After his defeats for the presidency in 1896, 1900 and 1908, in which he blamed the political control of the brewers for his increasing loss of big-city votes, Bryan became an all-out advocate of prohibition. He warned his listeners that there was no room for compromise and no middle ground. "This is a moral question," he thundered. "There is but one side to a moral question. Which side do you take?"

When he became President Wilson's Secretary of State and banned all drinks but water and grape juice at official diplomatic functions, many wets laughed at him and called him a has-been from another age. But although his political power was almost gone by the time national prohibition finally was put before the voters, Bryan's personal influence and example helped create strong sentiment for the drys.

Among the many other speakers who helped swing public opinion against the saloons, few drew larger audiences than evangelist Billy Sunday. His religious revival meetings stirred entire cities to emotional hysteria as he passionately denounced "that stinking, dirty, rotten, Hell-soaked business." Breezy, slangy and informal, he dazzled listeners with his showmanship and worked harder than any actor to dramatize every word he spoke. He would slap his head, grab one foot in his hand and hop about on the other, hold his nose, make faces, leap into the air, pound his feet, run, jump, race back and forth on the platform, fall to his knees or throw himself face-down with a thud. Ripping off his coat to stand in his shirtsleeves, drenched with sweat, he would suddenly drop his voice to a whisper, or roar out with rage.

When some of the clergy criticized him for coarse and undignified sermons, he said, "What do I care if some puff-eyed, dainty little dibbly-dibbly preacher goes tibbly-tibbing around because I use plain Anglo-Saxon words? I want people to know what I mean, and I try to get down to where

73

they live." He deliberately provoked controversy, and one of his favorite stunts was to line up a row of handsome young boys on the platform and offer them as "one day's contribution to the saloon's grist of manhood."

A son of Iowa pioneers, he was born in a log cabin in 1862, was put in an orphanage after his father died in the Civil War and never had much formal education. "I am a rube of the rubes," he once said. "I am a hayseed of the hayseeds." By the time he was twenty, earning his own living at unskilled labor in Marshalltown, Iowa, Billy Sunday also had become something of a local celebrity as a sandlot baseball player. Discovered by a major league scout, he became a star fielder for the Chicago White Sox, and later with Pittsburgh and Philadelphia teams. Never a great hitter, he struck out his first thirteen times at bat, but he did become a champion base-stealer, the fastest runner in the National League and a baseball hero. Traveling around the circuit, having a good time and living high, he also became a heavy drinker, and the habit worried him.

His conversion to the religious life came one day in Chicago, after he and some of his teammates had been out elbow-bending in a saloon. "It was a Sunday afternoon, and we got tanked up and then went and sat on a corner," he later recalled. Across the street there was an outdoor preacher and a religious band playing and singing "gospel hymns that I used to hear my mother sing back in the log cabin in Iowa." When one of the band invited him to come along to services at a nearby mission, mistaking him for a drunken bum, his baseball pals kidded him, but he decided to go. "I turned and left that little group on the corner," he said, "and walked to the little mission and fell on my knees and staggered out of sin."

Billy Sunday went on playing baseball for a time, but he also began speaking out for his newfound religion, and he attracted audiences because of his fame as a sports star. Finally he quit playing ball to work for the Y.M.C.A., and then to become an assistant to an evangelist who staged tent revival meetings in the Midwest. He branched out on his own and, as he gained prominence, moved into large Eastern cities with week-long revival meetings that drew huge crowds and made him a national figure.

With a traveling staff of some fifty advance men, publicists, top musicians, choir directors, hymn writers and even a master carpenter who supervised the construction of great wooden tabernacles, his activities began weeks before he arrived in a city. There would be as many as four thousand advance neighborhood prayer meetings to whip up enthusiasm for his coming. Newspapers would print special editions, and local clubs, schools, churches, business and fraternal organizations all would be involved.

His temporary tabernacles were big barns of unpainted timber. Above the platform was a huge sounding board, shaped like a giant flour scoop, to carry his voice, and behind the platform was a post office, a press room, telephones for reporters, a nursery where babies could be left and an emergency hospital with a nurse in attendance. Sunday and his staff would rent a whole house to set up as headquarters.

Brewers spent money liberally to fight his influence. They moved agents into cities ahead of him to spread rumors about his personal life, to arouse the resistance and to try to disrupt meetings. In Scranton, when a Billy Sunday Week ended with a street parade of dry converts, a mob tried to break it up by racing a big brewery wagon into the line of march. Sunday's temperance followers overturned the wagon and sent its beer kegs rolling into the street. The incident inspired one of the most popular songs of his career, "De Brewer's Big Horses Can't Run Over Me." It had an enormous sheet music sale, and thousands of militant followers across the country lifted their voices to sing about the brewer's horses that were "toting Lucifer's load."

During a battle in Illinois for local option laws, he toured by special train, and thirteen of the fifteen towns in which he campaigned voted out the saloon. He also campaigned through Western towns where liquor laws were at issue. "Whiskey is all right in its place," he told audiences, "but its place is Hell" and "the way to get rid of drunkards is to quit raising drunkards—to put the business that makes drunkards out of business."

A far more violent enemy of the saloons was hatchet-wielding Carry Amelia Nation. Probably more than any other individual, she kept the limelight of public attention focused on the worst evils of the saloons at a time when they could least afford the notoriety. Her raging saloon-smashing raids and her fury against the liquor trade kept her on the front pages of the nation's newspapers for more than ten years. Although many made fun of her as a comic figure and called her a madwoman, she dramatically carried out the secret wishes of a growing number of Americans who also wanted to see the saloons destroyed.

A religious fanatic, subject to wild dreams, spells, visions and hallucinations from earliest childhood, Carry Nation blamed liquor for all her personal woes, of which she had many, and for the mental illness of her grandmother, mother and several cousins, aunts and uncles and of her own daughter. She herself finally died in a Kansas hospital in 1911 of "nervous trouble."

On the Kentucky farm where she was born in 1846, her first recollections were of a mother who became convinced she was the Queen of England, to the point of dressing in regal gowns, wearing a cut-glass crown and riding about the countryside in a "royal coach" to command "her subjects." Carry's father, George Moore, who indulged his wife's whims, was a prosperous slaveholding planter and stock trader, but also a roving adventurer who led the family over a good part of pioneer Kentucky and Texas before finally settling in Missouri when Carry was sixteen.

She was a sickly girl, forever beset by troubles and misfortunes, and her first husband, a young Missouri doctor, developed the same heavy drinking habits she attributed to her own family, and died a helpless drunkard. She taught school and then married a lawyer, David Nation. He didn't drink, but was unsuccessful at the practice of law, and while she ran frontier rooming houses to try to keep them out of poverty, he became an equally improvident preacher. He eventually divorced her, after she began to gain national notoriety and he became jealous of the attention she was receiving.

Carry Nation was near her mid-fifties, living with her husband in the little village of Medicine Lodge, Kansas, having daydreams of terrifying hand-to-hand combat with Satan and of personal talks with God, when she received what she believed was divine inspiration to destroy the saloons. She said later that the very fact that her father had misspelled the name "Carrie" as "Carry" when she was christened was an omen, and that Carry A. Nation meant she was destined to become "the roused heart and conscience of the people" in their determination to "carry a nation" in attacking the saloon.

She carried no hatchet or other weapons at first. She hoped to conquer the saloons with prayer, by reviving the methods that had been successful during the Woman's Crusade twenty-five years before. Since Kansas was under state prohibition and all its drinking places were illegal speakeasies, she held that citizens had a perfect right to drive them out of business. In 1899, she started her prayer crusade, with the help of the county W.C.T.U., of which she was president, and in less than a year closed the speakeasies of Medicine Lodge and drove the bootleggers out of town.

But the next summer, when she turned her attention to the then wicked nearby town of Kiowa, and failed to persuade the saloonkeepers with prayers and hymn-singing, Carry Nation adopted more drastic methods. In a rage, she marched into three speakeasies, one after the other, and smashed up the places, shattering bottles, kegs and fixtures and creating a great excitement that brought newspaper correspondents rushing to the scene. Soon the whole country was reading about her saloon-smashing exploits.

In Wichita, the second largest city in Kansas, she dropkicked a brass cuspidor at a saloonkeeper's head, hurled bricks and paving stones through other saloon windows and smashed mirrors and rows of bottles with an iron bar. When she totally ruined the most ornate and fashionable speakeasy in the city, she finally was arrested for destroying property and was put in jail. But as soon as lawyers managed to get her released, she took up the attack once more. After delivering an impassioned talk at a women's temperance gathering, she went to the home of one of the women to gather up weapons, and in the family tool chest found the shining hatchet that was to become the symbol of her crusades.

Carrying the hatchet in the crook of her arm, she led a force of women into battle. The others also had weapons concealed under their long cloaks—pieces of scrap iron, clubs and stones wrapped in newspaper—and they marched through the streets singing "Onward Christian Soldiers." When a bartender blocked the entrance to James Burnes's saloon and tried to talk the ladies out of their warlike mission, Carry brandished her hatchet. "Out of my way, you rummy!" she cried, as she brought it sweeping down past his ear. "How dare you interfere with God's work?"

He yelled in fright, ran to the rear of the room and hid

under a table while the smashers went to work. Carry shattered the plate-glass window and the door, and started chopping up the bar with her hatchet. The others made havoc of the bottles and decanters. Her final blow with the hatchet cracked the expensive bar mirror into splinters. When there was nothing left to smash, they stood in the center of the room and Carry raised her right hand high. "Peace on earth," she said. "Goodwill to men."

Followed by a growing crowd, she and her feminine avengers went on to wreck other saloons. A week later, she led a similar band in attacks on the speakeasies of Topeka, the state capital, causing so much damage that the police were finally forced to arrest her, much to the embarrassment of state officials, who didn't want to admit publicly that there was any illegal liquor being sold in Kansas. From then on, Carry Nation raged up and down the state smashing speakeasies. She carried her "hatchetation" to other parts of the country, creating an uproar wherever she appeared.

The Anti-Saloon League ignored her, but she became a heroine of women's temperance groups, lecturing or hatcheting. Her denunciations of the liquor trade were as savage as her saloon-smashing. Arrested many times, clubbed, beaten, stoned, splashed with eggs and rotten vegetables, threatened with lynching, she also had a good following of sympathizers and was hardly ever out of the news. In many cities reporters took her on tours of the saloons and goaded her into actions that would make fresh headlines. She sold thousands of small souvenir hatchets, ran a newspaper called *The Smasher's Mail,* and became the subject of songs, books, humorists and cartoonists.

Saloonkeepers, except for those whose places fell under her hatchet, generally treated Carry Nation as the biggest joke of the century. They thought it was uproariously funny to concoct drinks named for her and to hang signs over their bars that read: "All Nations Welcome but Carry." But everything said against her only increased the publicity that made the saloon a constant American eyesore. A zealot she was, but legally insane she was never proved to be, and her hatchet swung with it the feelings of many who delighted in her crusades.

The Wild West hero the drys claimed in support of their cause, William Eugene Johnson, better known as "Pussyfoot" Johnson, once boasted that as the Anti-Saloon League's agent in charge of "underground activities" he had lied, bribed and drunk gallons of liquor to trick his enemies and help put over prohibition. Years after prohibition became a fact, he proudly admitted that "the lies I have told would fill a big book."

He started out as a country school teacher, not far from the farm at Coventry, New York, where he was born in 1862, but while he was still a young man he quit the schoolhouse and headed West to Nebraska. There he worked as a cowboy on a ranch near Fremont, put himself through three years at Nebraska State University, ran a weekly newspaper and a Turkish bath and made and lost a small fortune as a land speculator in town lots before he married and settled down for a brief time as a newspaper correspondent.

As a reporter and an ardent temperance man, Johnson had learned his hatred of liquor from his strict Presbyterian parents, and he soon was in the thick of the battle in 1889, when the drys began organizing for a fight to make prohibition part of Nebraska's constitution. Posing as a liquor dealer to win the confidence of the wets, he produced sensational evidence of payoffs and corruption and won the attention of national temperance leaders.

Johnson had become a Washington lobbyist for the drys by 1906, when Congress decided it was time to clean up the lawlessness in the Indian Territories and Oklahoma, where shootings, lynchings, gambling and the illegal liquor trade were getting out of hand. There were few marshals; criminals from other parts of the Union had sought refuge there, and the territorial prohibition laws were being openly defied. Twenty-five thousand dollars was appropriated for an effort to wipe out the liquor trade, in the hope of ending the connected crime, and the Commissioner of Indian Affairs named Johnson as a special officer to take charge.

With the federal government paying expenses, Johnson chose his own staff and arrived in Tulsa in great secrecy. He mapped out the trouble spots of what then was still a small town and, in a series of surprise raids that struck a dozen places at once, all but put the bootleggers out of business within a week.

As he moved on into the surrounding area, dumping liquor, making arrests and trailing down suspects in true Wild West fashion, he became known as the "Booze Buster." Johnson donned a broad-brimmed cowboy hat and a long coat, and took to carrying a rifle. National newspaper cartoonists began picturing him, gun in hand, fighting the demon rum, and his fame quickly spread. He halted shipments into the Indian territory by putting an agent at every rail station to seize consignments of liquor as they arrived, led his men into express offices to break thousands of bottles, staged hundreds of lightning strikes against speakeasies. Johnson was constantly threatened and shot at, and at least eight of his men were gunned down.

When one saloonkeeper threatened to shoot him on sight, Johnson disguised himself, walked into the place pretending to be drunk, and slapped a silver dollar on the bar. When the man leaned close to serve the drink, Johnson put a gun to his ear and led him out under arrest. A newspaper account of what happened gave him the nickname "Pussyfoot" by referring to Johnson as "the velvet-shod emissary of

Uncle Sam's booze department . . . he of the panther tread." Outlaws offered three thousand dollars to any man who would kill him.

At another place, where he smashed open the door in a surprise raid, men tried to dive out the window to an adjoining roof, but he backed them off and herded them up by firing shots at their feet. During eleven months, he and his deputies hauled more than five hundred men into court, including five who were charged with murder, made 902 seizures of liquor, destroyed 72,000 gallons of beer and whiskey and confiscated horses, wagons, saddles and other property, selling it at government auction.

He was promoted to Chief Special Officer of the Commission of Indian Affairs, to take charge of suppressing the liquor traffic on all Indian reservations throughout the United States, and his headquarters was moved from Oklahoma to Salt Lake City. Congress doubled its appropriation of money, and as Johnson led his men into Indian lands in New Mexico, Idaho and California, a Chicago newspaper reported that since he had taken over, "a whirlwind has been playing havoc among the whiskey peddlers of the Indian reservations west of the Rocky Mountains."

Johnson was involved in a dozen knock-down fights, a knife attack and two shooting frays in Montana, where he piled up so many arrests that special grand juries had to be called in to handle the cases. In California, he trailed a desperado sixty miles into the desert, captured him and led him back to jail. By 1911, Johnson and his men had made some six thousand arrests and had won court convictions in most of the cases, but he quarreled with new bosses in Washington, and when they accused him of insubordination he resigned.

He soon was in command of the Anti-Saloon League's publishing plant, planning and editing the flood of propaganda that came from it, and also acting as an organizer, agent and political strategist. As the real fight for national prohibition moved closer, there were books to be written, economic studies to be made, funds to be raised and states to be organized, and "Pussyfoot" Johnson had a hand in all of them.

8

The Anti-Saloon League, still carefully building its political power step by step, had not yet come out for national prohibition. But in the years before the First World War it turned a good part of the nation dry. It won hundreds of political contests in cities and counties and organized its voter strength so solidly in both major parties that it held the balance of power in a growing number of state legislatures. In some states a lawmaker who ignored the League's demands risked almost certain political ruin.

When the twentieth century began, state-wide prohibition was in effect in only three states: Maine, Kansas and North Dakota. The League and the groups working with it started a new wave of state prohibition by turning Georgia dry in 1907, followed the same year by Oklahoma. The next year, Mississippi and North Carolina voted for state prohibition, and in 1909 Tennessee joined the ranks. West Virginia was next in 1912, and in 1914, Virginia, Oregon, Washington, Colorado and Arizona went dry. The prohibition wave rolled on until there were twenty-six dry states by the time the United States entered the First World War, and thirty-three had chosen state prohibition before national prohibition became law.

But the new wave of state prohibition found its strength mainly in agricultural and small-town America and in states where legislatures were dominated by rural lawmakers. A highly populated belt of the nation, including big cities and industrial areas of the North and East, remained wet. In addition, many of the so-called dry states were far from being bone-dry. Only thirteen totally prohibited all manufacture and sale of liquor. Instead of full prohibition, the laws were aimed mostly at abolishing the saloon and bringing the liquor trade under strict control.

Despite the new wave of state prohibition, Americans were drinking more than ever. Liquor flowed freely into dry states and counties from across their borders. One of the big leaks was in mail order sales. Liquor dealers in other states used circulars and newspaper advertisements to solicit orders, and Senator William Kenyon of Iowa charged that dry states were being deluged with "daily trainloads of liquor in bottles, jugs and other packages, consigned to persons real and fictitious, and every railway station and every express company office . . . are converted into the most extensive and active whiskey shops." Some mail order liquor sellers boldly advertised: "Uncle Sam is our partner."

The Anti-Saloon League drew up a proposed law, which Senator Kenyon and North Carolina's Representative Edwin Webb put before congress, designed to give states instead of the federal government control over liquor shipped across state boundaries. It became the first national test of the League's political power, and the drys won a far greater victory than they had expected.

The Webb-Kenyon bill was overwhelmingly passed. But the real measure of the League's strength in congress came after President William Howard Taft vetoed the act. Taft called it unconstitutional and declared that "it clearly violates the commerce clause of our fundamental law." But congress stood with the Anti-Saloon League against the president and early in 1913 passed the law over Taft's vote by more than a two-thirds majority of both House and Senate.

Wets admitted the vote was "the handwriting on the wall that spells doom," and the League jubilantly turned almost at once to start the battle for national prohibition. In all the years it had been building its power in the states the League had carefully avoided taking a stand for national prohibition. But after the success in congress of the Webb-Kenyon law, a secret poll of dry leaders throughout the country convinced League officials that the time finally had come to act.

Among those who made the strongest pleas for immediate action was the League's attorney, Wayne B. Wheeler. A brilliant and hard-working man in his early forties, with a hunger for personal power, Wheeler was to become the driving force behind the movement, absolute boss of the League and the unofficial czar of prohibition.

As an Ohio farm boy he had taught country school and worked as a waiter and janitor to earn his way through college at Oberlin, then a center of the Ohio temperance movement. Wheeler became interested in the Anti-Saloon League from its very beginning in Ohio; he attended its first public meeting and accepted a part-time job while still in college to help the League's founder, the Reverend Howard Russell. When he graduated, he gave up the promise of a sales career to become a full-time agent of the Ohio League, and moved upward with it as it grew into a national organization. He studied law and became the League's national attorney as well as its organizer and general trouble-shooter. Others were still in command of League affairs when it began the fight for national prohibition, but Wayne Wheeler was determined to push both the League and himself to greater power.

Hundreds of League delegates from all parts of the country made their way through a blizzard to Columbus, Ohio, in the second week in November, 1913, for a twenty-year Jubilee Convention. Former Governor J. Frank Hanly of Indiana made a stirring speech in favor of a resolution for national prohibition, and the convention adopted it with wild enthusiasm and without a dissenting vote. "The convention cut loose with a roar as wild as the raging storm outside," Wheeler wrote. "It jumped to its feet and yelled approval. The first shot in the battle for the Eighteenth Amendment had been fired."

One month later, five thousand men and women summoned to Washington for a demonstration by the Anti-Saloon League and the W.C.T.U., paraded up Pennsylvania Avenue. Wearing white satin badges and carrying banners, they sang a prophetic song that demanded "A Saloonless Nation by 1920," the three-hundredth anniversary of the landing of the Pilgrims. On the Capitol steps, they presented petitions to Senator Morris Sheppard of Texas and Representative Richmond P. Hobson of Alabama, asking congress to submit a Constitutional prohibition amendment to the states. The same day, Sheppard and Hobson introduced the League's resolution into both the Senate and the House.

Drafted with Wheeler's help as the League's attorney, the resolution for a change in the Constitution was the work of many men and none of the temperance groups was entirely satisfied with its terms, but they agreed to support it as a first step toward prohibition. The League made no attempt to bring it out of committee for a year. Before there was any vote, the drys wanted to be sure of their strength in congress. The League went to work to win that strength in the congressional elections of 1914. It spent nearly three million dollars in the campaign.

"Back of the drive were virtually all the Protestant denominations," Wheeler later wrote, "and through the churches of the country the Washington headquarters was in close touch with every section of the United States. Through the state leagues, which directed the campaign locally, we were at all times intimately in touch with the battle on all fronts." The League also meant "to let Congress hear from the people back home," and the letters, telegrams and petitions "rolled in by the tens of thousands."

"We started off with about 20,000 speakers, mostly volunteers, all over the United States," Wheeler recalled. "They spoke at every opportunity, at every sort of gathering. . . . During the final stages of the battle there were approximately 50,000 trained speakers, volunteers and regulars, directing their fire upon the wets in every village, town, city, county and state." The League's printing plant at Westerville "ran three shifts a day, every hour of the twenty-four, grinding out dry literature," and the League "went into every congressional district where there was a chance to elect a dry and waged as strong a fight as candidates have ever seen."

When the 1914 election returns were counted, the drys had "triumphed even beyond our hopes," as Wheeler put it. They gained many seats. They knew they still lacked enough votes to command a Constitutional two-thirds majority in both houses, but they decided to make a trial run to determine what still had to be done. The Hobson resolution was brought out of the Judiciary Committee to the floor of the House, and on December 22, 1914, congress began its first classic debate over whether prohibition should be made part of the Constitution.

More than one hundred brief speeches were made in the House, under an agreement that limited the time for each and divided it between wets and drys, in a continuous session that lasted from ten-thirty in the morning until eleven at night. When the vote was taken, the House was almost evenly divided, 197 in favor of prohibition to 190 against. The dry lead of seven votes was far less than the two-thirds majority required for an amendment to the Constitution; but it was a majority of congress, and even if the resolution hadn't passed, the Anti-Saloon League had demonstrated its power.

Stunned by the results, the wets expected the drys to make another try to push through the Amendment in 1915 and again in 1916, and each year made elaborate plans to fight it down. But the Anti-Saloon League deliberately avoided another showdown in congress until it was positive it had gained enough voting strength for certain success. It intended to run no risk of failure that might delay passage for years.

"The strategy of the day dictated holding off, so far as rushing congress was concerned," Wheeler wrote, "but back in the field, we did get busy again. All the energy we had put into the 1914 campaign boiled and bubbled with hotter fire into the campaign of 1916." It was during that campaign, before America entered the First World War, that prohibition was all but decided. Prohibition was a major issue before the voters in every contest across the country. "We knew late election night that we had won," Wheeler claimed. "We knew that the prohibition amendment would be submitted to the states by the Congress just elected."

But whether the League could have put across prohibition if the United States hadn't become involved in the First World War is a question still debated. Wartime hysteria changed the whole atmosphere of public opinion. The League capitalized on the war in every way possible to convince the nation that the emergency demanded prohibition as an act of patriotism, to help speed victory and to create the sort of a morally clean country to which its fighting heroes should return.

Wets charged later that prohibition was "put over on the country" while most of its men were away fighting the war. But the fact is that the decisive elections of 1916 came five months before America entered the war and more than a year before soldiers reached the European fighting front. Another charge was that women voted prohibition into law while men were off fighting, but in most of the country women still had no right to vote. Nevertheless, the war at least greatly hastened the adoption of the Eighteenth Amendment and its swift ratification by the states.

From the moment war first broke out in Europe in 1914, there was strong feeling against the Germans, and many brewers were German-Americans. The drys began an unceasing campaign of propaganda to ban beer as un-American and to picture the entire brewing industry as spies, traitors and "murderous Huns." After America entered the war in 1917, hatred of everything German became an emotional frenzy. Saloons were suspected of harboring nests of saboteurs or enemy agents, and people were terrified by false rumors that germ warfare was being spread in poisonous beer. League propagandists claimed that it was German troops under the influence of alcohol who committed alleged war atrocities and that beer and German militarism went together.

The League helped inspire a senate investigation that revealed a link between brewing interests and the German-American Alliance, first founded around the turn of the century to promote German culture in the United States. The brewers had helped subsidize it as a front for anti-prohibition campaigning, but when war came the Alliance was denounced for spreading anti-American propaganda, and the senate hearings produced black headlines. Another sensational investigation brought federal anti-trust charges against brewers for conspiring to violate state and national laws through vote-buying, bribery and hidden control of newspapers and magazines. A grand jury indicted two brewers' associations and a large number of corporations associated with the industry. Some pleaded guilty and paid fines totaling $100,000.

Much was also made of the patriotic argument that grain wasted in the making of alcohol would provide millions of loaves of bread to feed America and its fighting European allies. Another dry argument was that brewers and distillers took thousands of men from home-front jobs vital to war production, used trucks and trains needed for the transportation of war materials and put a burden on the whole of industry that should be geared for war.

As the Anti-Saloon League aimed its sights on the incoming 1917 congress that had been elected in the 1916 campaign, League leaders were fully confident that they could get a prohibition amendment whenever they wanted it. But they carefully avoided overconfidence. They knew they had to keep public opinion behind them all the way. There were still many tricky political traps to avoid and much trading and dealing to be done before the Amendment could be brought through.

9

When President Woodrow Wilson called the new congress into special session in the spring of 1917 to declare a state of war with Germany, Senator Morris Sheppard of Texas lost little time in introducing the Anti-Saloon League's resolution to add a prohibition amendment to the Constitution. It was referred to the Senate Judiciary Committee, where it stayed three months while congress was busy enacting vital war legislation. President Wilson had appealed to the League to agree to the delay, and the League was willing. It used those months for hard bargaining with the wets to help ease the Eighteenth Amendment safely through congress.

The wets had all but given up hope of keeping congress from passing the Amendment along to the states, but they were confident that ratification battles in the states would keep it from ever becoming part of the Constitution. Drys would need to win majorities in both houses of thirty-six state legislatures, but wets would need a majority in only one house of thirteen state legislatures to block ratification, and the wets boasted that they could delay prohibition for years and hold out that many states forever if they had to. What alarmed brewers and distillers far more was a move launched by the drys for immediate wartime prohibition to shut down the liquor industry through an emergency act of congress.

When the drys attached a rider to a food control bill to prohibit the use of grain and other foodstuffs for the manufacture of alcoholic beverages, wets in the Senate threatened a filibuster and President Wilson intervened to keep the action from blocking necessary wartime food controls. He got League officials to accept a rewritten version of the food bill, but the drys continued to hold the threat of immediate wartime prohibition over the brewers and distillers to gain every compromise they could.

Some wet leaders let it be known that they would drop their objections to congressional passage of the Eighteenth Amendment if the drys would drop their pressure for wartime prohibition, and a deal finally was made on those terms. With the wets lulled into believing there was no immediate danger that brewers would be put out of business the Eighteenth Amendment had clear sailing when it reached the floor of the Senate at the end of July, 1917. During thirteen hours of debate that stretched over three days, the drys easily defeated several attempts to weaken the Amendment and on August 1, the Senate passed it by a vote of sixty-five to twenty.

When the battle shifted to the House, the drys made another trade with the wets. In return for a year's grace for the liquor trade to wind up its affairs if the Amendment did get ratified by the states, the wets agreed to allow more time for ratification. The new terms were that the Amendment would have to be approved by the states within seven years and that prohibition would go into effect one year after ratification.

By the time the Eighteenth Amendment reached the House, the dramatic events of the war had all but overshadowed prohibition. Many congressmen, tired of being under pressure by the League and by voters back home, and knowing that passage was a foregone conclusion, simply wanted to get it over with. The House gave it even less time than the Senate and wrapped the whole thing up in one day. Debate began shortly before noon on December 18, 1917, and after a six-hour rehearing of old arguments, the House voted 282 to 128 to submit the Eighteenth Amendment to the states.

The Amendment was hardly out of congress and on its way to the state legislatures before the Anti-Saloon League renewed its fight to put the brewers out of business with immediate wartime prohibition. To those who charged them with bad faith and accused them of going back on their promises, drys answered that they were acting in the patriotic spirit of what was best for the nation. In their view, prohibition would help win the war and preserve the peace, and they meant to turn America dry even before the states ratified the Eighteenth Amendment.

They finally pushed through a wartime prohibition law that wasn't enacted until November 21, 1918, ten days after the signing of the Armistice in Europe. Although the war was then over and the emergency ended, congressional approval at a time when the states were considering the Eighteenth Amendment linked the cause of prohibition with the new aims of peace. Dry propaganda preached that closing the breweries was all part of the dream for a better America, where liquor would be forever banished and evil and corruption would be driven from the land.

The battle for ratification in the states turned out to be

no battle at all. Wets who were sure it would drag on for at least seven years had failed to take into account the fact that the Anti-Saloon League had been working in the states for almost a quarter of a century, building its strength through lobbyists in every state capitol and political back room. Veterans of hundreds of state political wars, its highly trained and skilled agents were backed by an efficient central organization, thousands of volunteers, as much money as they needed and a propaganda mill that had never ceased fire. With the American flag wrapped around prohibition, the churches behind it and the people brought up for generations to believe that the saloon was the center of all evil, it would have been surprising if the Eighteenth Amendment had failed. But even the League was surprised by the speed with which the states embraced national prohibition.

Mississippi was the first state to ratify, on January 8, 1918, and by early January, 1919, a little more than a year after ratification began, thirty-five states had approved. Only in five was the vote even close. Before the rush to jump aboard the wagon ended, more than eighty per cent of the members of all the state legislatures in the nation had voted in favor of prohibition.

At 10:32 on the morning of January 16, the Nebraska legislature almost unanimously voted its approval, and with three-quarters of the states in line, ratification was complete. In Washington, the Eighteenth Amendment was procalimed part of the Constitution, and the official announcement was made that prohibition would go into effect everywhere in the United States one year from that date. Afterward, twelve more states ratified and only two, Connecticut and Rhode Island, finally refused.

That the hastily adopted Eighteenth Amendment had many flaws soon became apparent, but critics said that its basic flaw was that it dealt with only one side of the liquor problem. Americans were still perfectly free to buy liquor, to use it and to keep it in their homes without breaking the law or facing any penalty. The threat of putting the seller in jail meant nothing to the buyer, who ran no risk at all, and many good citizens would go right on drinking, able to ease their consciences because the Amendment included no clause against the purchase of alcohol.

Those who tried to plan its enforcement were faced with a fundamental conflict. Other parts of the Constitution guaranteed Americans certain rights, such as security of their persons, homes and effects against unreasonable search and seizure, speedy and impartial public trial, immunity from being forced to become witnesses against themselves and a heritage of other basic liberties which many people felt that the enforcement of the Eighteenth Amendment might violate. Dry leaders realized that if they hoped to keep the nation from resisting prohibition, or from becoming too aroused over the invasion of individual rights, they had to frame enforcement laws that would be a compromise between what was desired and what was politically possible. Enforcement had to be neither too terrifying nor too weak.

Attorney Wayne Wheeler had been working for months before the Eighteenth Amendment was ratified to draw up a rough draft of the enforcement laws the Anti-Saloon League wanted. He gathered material from all the dry states on their experiences in trying to enforce state prohibition, added suggestions made by a special committee of the League and finally produced the National Prohibition Act, which he turned over to House Judiciary Committee Chairman Andrew J. Volstead of Minnesota. The law became known as the Volstead Act, although Volstead did little more than rearrange some sections of the bill Wheeler handed him to introduce. Wheeler also had the League provide the Judiciary Committee and other "friends in congress" with information sheets because "many of them do not know what laws are needed or the precedents and reasons for them."

The House Judiciary Committee did water down some originally severe clauses that dealt with search and seizure, with soliciting orders for liquor and with requiring local officers to report arrests for drunkeness. When the Act came before the House itself in October, 1919, amendments were tacked on to allow for the possession of liquor in private homes and the sale of sacramental wine, and to provide heavy penalties against the wrongful issue of search warrants. With the drys in full command there was no real challenge, and only a few congressmen bothered to take part in the debate before the House adopted the Volstead Act 287 to 100.

The Senate, in committee hearings and through amendments, made other changes, mainly to make sure people would be allowed to consume and store as much liquor as they wished in "residences, apartments, hotels and similar places of abode," and to permit farmers and others to make light wine and cider at home. After two days of listless debate, the Senate approved the Volstead Act without even the formality of a roll-call vote, and details were then worked out in joint conference with the House.

In its final form, it was an act of seventy-three sections that filled twenty closely printed pages with a complicated maze of legal technicalities, to the deep confusion of most of those who would try to enforce it. Basically it prohibited the manufacture, sale, barter, transport, import, export, delivery or illegal possession of any intoxicating beverage, with certain exceptions. "Intoxicating" was defined as one-half of one per cent of alcohol by volume. Permits were to be issued for the manufacture of industrial alcohol, and for alcohol for medicinal, religious and other specialized uses. The most curious feature of the Volstead Act was that although the war had been over for some eight months, it provided for the enforcement not only of the Eighteenth Amendment but also of immediate wartime prohibition. In effect, although it generally was ignored in practice, it would have wiped out the Eighteenth Amendment's own condition that the liquor trade would have a year to wind up its business.

President Wilson decided that was too much. He had kept his hands off the fight over prohibition, but to the astonishment of the Anti-Saloon League and of congress, he vetoed the Volstead Act on October 27. Wilson pointed out in his veto message that the war emergency had long since passed and that he believed the wartime prohibition should be repealed. "In all matters having to do with the personal habits and customs of large numbers of our people, we must be certain that the established processes of legal change are followed," he wrote. "In no other way can the salutary object sought to be accomplished by great reforms of this character be made satisfactory and permanent."

Although he did not directly express either approval or disapproval of prohibition, there were those who read into his rather cryptic veto message an implied criticism of the Eighteenth Amendment. It was a point long to be debated by historians, but it made little difference. Within two hours of the time President Wilson sent his message to congress, the House overrode his veto, and the Senate the next day did the same.

The Noble Experiment, in the making for centuries, was about to begin, and the great majority of Americans wishfully saw in the coming of prohibition the eternal promise the drys had made to them of a gloriously happy, prosperous and crime-free land.

Church bells rang throughout the land as prohibition began at one minute past midnight on January 17, 1920. John Barleycorn, the make-believe figure who symbolized drink, was proclaimed officially dead. Ten thousand drys turned out for the mock funeral service staged in Norfolk, Virginia, by showman Billy Sunday. John Barleycorn's "body," in a twenty-foot casket, was drawn by horses and escorted by twenty gleeful pallbearers to the evangelist's tabernacle.

"Good-bye, John. You were God's worst enemy. You were Hell's best friend," Sunday shouted, while a group of actors pretending to be victims of liquor wailed from a mourner's bench and a man dressed in the devil's suit of Satan hopped about. "The reign of tears is over. The slums will soon be only a memory. We will turn our prisons into factories and our jails into storehouses and corncribs. Men will walk upright now, women will smile, and children will laugh. Hell will be forever for rent."

Congregations in Protestant churches everywhere held watch-night and thanksgiving services. There were parades, demonstrations, mass meetings and some more elaborate ceremonies that went on for several days. The W.C.T.U. called for meetings in every city and town where it had a chapter. Temperance delegates from all parts of the United States attended a watch-night service in Washington to celebrate the start of a "Happy Dry Year" and to hear the rousing oratory of William Jennings Bryan. The Anti-Saloon League confidently predicted "an era of clear thinking and clean living" in which "a new nation will be born," and its New York superintendent, William Anderson, appealed to wets to "be good sports" and to accept the fact that prohibition was the law of the land. "Shake hands with Uncle Sam," he urged, "and board his water wagon."

Newspapers predicted that the last night before prohibition would produce the greatest orgy of drinking the country had ever seen, but they were wrong. While there were some elaborate parties, the expected final binge fizzled out and prohibition came in quietly. Even on the last "wet" New Year's Eve, New York was gripped by a snowstorm, and midnight found the streets all but empty and even Times Square uncrowded. In smaller towns and villages many would-be celebrants discovered saloons already dry or serving only soft drinks. Most saloonkeepers had been busy trying to sell out all they had before prohibition closed their doors.

But since the start of the Christmas holidays and even before, people had been drinking up or hoarding all the liquor they could find. Demand had sent prices soaring. Some drinkers had seemed in near-panic. Hundreds of motorists made a wild dash into the wine-producing area of New York State hoping to buy the last bottles of champagne, driving through snow-clogged roads that stranded many of them so they had to be rescued by highway patrols. New Jerseyites stampeded to the banks of a river where a brewery dumped the last of its stock of beer. Many private clubs and individuals tried to lay in supplies of liquor, and some rented cellars, warehouses and bank safety-deposit boxes for storage. Liquor dealers ran advertisements urging people to "buy now," picturing a top-hatted Uncle Sam fiercely holding a gun, with the scare caption, "Uncle Sam will *enforce* prohibition!"

Two days before prohibition began, federal enforcement officials, backed by a court ruling, announced that all privately owned liquor in warehouses, safety-deposit boxes and other storage places would be liable to seizure as soon as the law went into effect. In New York, Chicago, San Francisco and other cities, people rushed out to hire trucks, moving vans, automobiles and horses and wagons to cart their hidden treasures to their homes, since private dwellings remained the only safe place to hoard liquor under the law.

Government officials also issued a reminder that any vehicle found transporting liquor when the law became effective would be subject to seizure. When one prohibition agent was asked what would happen if a man were caught carrying a hip flask, he told reporters that in such circumstances the man's pants would be considered a "vehicle," and would be subject to seizure. That produced a laugh, but at the start of prohibition there were few Americans who looked on the law as a joke. Almost everybody, wets and drys alike, expected it to be strictly, rigidly and easily enforced.

Few doubted the Anti-Saloon League's Wayne Wheeler when he predicted that after the first year enforcement would become a minor problem and that federal funds needed to make people obey the law probably could be reduced. Colonel Daniel Porter, supervising revenue agent in New

York, said that "there will not be any violations to speak of." With his enforcement organization ready to go to work, the nation's first Prohibition Commissioner, John F. Kramer, issued an optimistic statement in Washington that "this law will be obeyed in cities large and small."

The Department of Justice expected so few violations that it made no special preparations to handle court cases which might grow out of prohibition. A force of federal agents, fifteen hundred strong, backed by Coast Guard and Customs men, was set to go into action at midnight. Police of a thousand cities and sheriffs of a thousand counties were alerted to do their duty. With such a mighty fist of enforcement poised to strike at those who might risk disobedience, officials generally believed there would be little drinking in America.

Having made prohibition part of the Constitution, most drys considered their battle already won. They were confident that people would obey the law the way they obeyed all other laws, for the most part willingly, and that enforcement would be necessary to punish only those few who refused to accept the established rules of society. Wartime restrictions had already conditioned people to accepting federal regulation. Years of dry propaganda had promised that prohibition would produce the best of all possible worlds. Self-sacrifice and reform were the spirit of the day. Newspapers warned readers of the severe penalties and expressed little doubt that the law would be accepted.

There were, of course, some who did have doubts, but they were the minority. During the debates in congress over prohibition, a number of Senators and Representatives had predicted it would never work. Perhaps the most prophetic statement from any national figure came from former President William Howard Taft. He supported prohibition once it was enacted, but he clearly warned of what he believed would come.

"The business of manufacturing alcohol, liquor and beer will go out of the hands of law-abiding members of the community, and will be transferred to the quasi-criminal class," Taft said. "In the communities where the majority will not sympathize with a federal law's restrictions, a large number of federal officers will be needed for its enforcement. . . . The reaching out of this great central power to brush the doorsteps of local communities . . . will be irritating . . . and will be a strain upon the bond of the national union. It will produce variations in the enforcement of the law. There will be loose administration in spots all over the United States, and the politically inclined . . . will be strongly tempted to acquiesce in such a condition. . . ."

As the hour for prohibition neared, some states and large cities took the stand that, since they had no enforcement laws of their own, they intended to have no part in active enforcement, and would leave the task entirely to the small band of federal enforcers. Unofficially at least, police in many areas meant to look the other way and keep hands off. New Jersey's Governor Edward I. Edwards made his position clearer and declared that he hoped to keep New Jersey "as wet as the Atlantic Ocean."

The drys laughed at such statements. In their hour of triumph, they had full faith and no reservations about whether the law would dry up the country. They declared that the Eighteenth Amendment and the Volstead Act had effectively banished liquor forever. All that remained, they assured the American people, was a simple mopping-up operation.

Minutes after prohibition began, federal agents swung into operation. At 12:05 A.M., a saloonkeeper in Brooklyn,

New York, was caught serving a last glass of brandy and was arrested and held under $1000 bail. A Chinese restaurant in New York's Times Square area was raided. Warrants were issued for eleven other accused violators in the New York area, and there were token arrests in other cities. But there was no immediate big-scale crackdown. Enforcement officials thought it would be enough to show that they meant business and that people would take warning. The next day's newspapers reported that agents had seized trucks laden with liquor in New York and Peoria, Illinois. They had raided stills in Detroit and Hammond, Indiana.

Such arrests, raids and seizures soon became everyday happenings. From the first midnight on, there wasn't a minute, day or night, that the law was not flouted and violated, and as a flood of illegal liquor poured over the country the federal enforcers desperately tried one scheme after another in a helpless attempt to halt the flow. With never enough men or enough money, they had been given the impossible task of attempting to enforce a law that was riddled with a thousand loopholes for evasion.

In Chicago less than an hour after prohibition started, there was a foreshadowing of the challenge that was to come from the underworld. A gang of six masked men invaded a railroad switchyard, bound and gagged the yardmaster and a watchman, herded half a dozen other trainmen into a shed and hijacked $100,000 worth of medicinal liquor from two freight cars. Within weeks, more than one hundred other thefts of large quantities of liquor were reported, and it was later revealed that more than half a million dollars' worth of liquor had been looted from warehouses where it was being kept under government bond for medicinal use.

The first year of prohibition set the pattern for all the problems that were to come. Before the Volstead Act had been in effect six months, there were indications of most of the major troubles that would multiply through the years ahead.

Raids on stills increased more than one thousand per cent. The Customs Service soon informed congress that it wasn't adequately financed to meet the increasing problem of liquor being smuggled into the country and that only "an infinitesimal quantity" of smuggled liquor was being seized. Several federal enforcement agents and a deputy collector of Internal Revenue were arrested on charges of corruption. Roundups of druggists accused of selling medicinal liquor without doctors' prescriptions were begun, and in Chicago alone it was estimated that doctors themselves had issued at least 300,000 fake prescriptions for whiskey since the law became effective. Industrial alcohol companies were caught diverting alcohol to beverage uses.

Courts quickly became clogged with thousands of prohibition cases. In Chicago, some six hundred cases were awaiting trial. The Department of Justice reported that federal district attorneys throughout the country were protesting that they could not enforce the Volstead Act without additional funds and assistance. Some state legislatures refused to appropriate money to help with enforcement, and federal men said that they were being forced to carry the whole burden because state and city law officers were unwilling to cooperate.

Many of the nation's lawmakers and others high in public life failed to set an example for sobriety. A special train carrying the Massachusetts delegation to the Republican National Convention in Chicago in June was raided by prohibition agents, who seized its stock of liquor. A few weeks later San Francisco was reported wide open during the Democratic National Convention. Harvard's Dr. Charles Eliot complained in a public address in Boston that many of the country's "best people"—those of wealth, influence and social position—were doing "much to interfere with prohibition enforcement" all over the United States. By their refusal to obey the law, he warned, they were "teaching lawlessness, especially to the young men of the country."

But none of the dry leaders, and few wets, foresaw the upheaval that would put reformers in the minority and lawbreakers in the majority. The drys generally ignored the pattern of what was happening and continued to make optimistic statements. Federal enforcers hoped things would get better. Congress was reluctant to do anything, especially if it meant appropriating more money or tightening gaps in the law in a way that might annoy voters. Hardly anybody at the start expected that the "Noble Experiment" would fail.

Prohibition didn't stop anybody who wanted to drink. From its start until its end there was never any real lack of liquor to supply the demand. But it did make good liquor more difficult to obtain, and a nation suddenly thirstier than ever seemed willing to swallow almost anything that had alcohol in it. People drank millions of gallons of concoctions that were almost always raw, sometimes dangerous and occasionally deadly. Most of them were mixtures of poor alcohol, water and various flavorings.

Although thousands of cases of real liquor were smuggled across the borders, and thousands more were drained out of government warehouses, very little of it reached drinkers without being doctored along the way. One case of good whisky, mixed with raw alcohol and water, would make five cases of bootleg whiskey. Packaged so only an expert could tell it from the original, each case could be sold as the "real stuff." Even that kind was special. Most of what the bootleggers sold contained not a drop of real whiskey or gin, despite their constant claim that every bottle was "right off the boat." The main product of the illicit stills was not whiskey but alcohol. It was easier to make than liquor and brought more profit when supplied to those who stirred together the various mixtures that passed for whiskey or gin.

The moonshiners who made it got their name from the small hill-country operators who worked mainly at night, but the term came to include operators of all kinds of illegal stills, large and small, that spread by the thousands from border to border. They became the largest source of alcohol for bootleg liquor. During the first five years of prohibition, federal agents seized some 697,000 stills, and by 1927 they were raiding them at the rate of more than 170,000 a year. But government spokesmen admitted that for every still they closed down there were at least nine more in operation. They estimated that there were half a million people engaged in the illegal business of cooking alcohol.

Stills were everywhere—in cities, towns and villages, hidden on remote farms and in wooded mountain areas, in warehouses, tenement basements and apartment living rooms and behind cigar stores and delicatessens that served as fronts for them. Many were family operations, with father, mother and children all taking part in the business. The distilling apparatus often was makeshift, the work amateur and hurried and the surroundings filthy. The mash frequently was made of a blend of sugar, water, yeast and garbage, in addition to whatever else might happen to fall into the mixture.

With the entrance of the organized gangs, the production of moonshine alcohol became based on the growing corn sugar industry, and this at least improved the ingredients. During prohibition the production of corn sugar expanded almost ten times, which made many farmers as well as gangsters happy. Although there were always many independent moonshiners whose operations were too small to interest the big-shot criminals, most of the alcohol makers were taken over by the gangs. The gangs also began to operate much larger distilleries of their own, well protected by bribed agents, police and politicians. Most of the gangs, to promote business and also to keep customers alive, made at least a token attempt to filter poisons out of the alcohol they supplied.

The second biggest source of illegal alcohol for making what passed for whiskey or gin came from the nation's industrial chemical industry. After the war there was an enormous growth in the legitimate chemical industry, and it was government policy to encourage expanding new factories that required alcohol for many products. The Volstead Act was carefully worded to allow for such use, but it also opened the floodgates that poured out millions of gallons of denatured alcohol bootleggers tried to convert into the kind people could drink. Industrial alcohol, manufactured by licensed distilleries in nineteen states, was passed through a denaturing process to make it unfit to drink. According to various formulas, any of some seventy-six substances might be added —some comparatively harmless, but others strong poisons. After being denatured, it was stored in government warehouses for sale under permit to companies that needed it for manufacturing.

To get a permit, an applicant was supposed to present reasonable proof that he had a legitimate use for it, but thousands of new chemical companies sprang up, many backed by bootleggers or the gangs, that never manufactured anything at all. They just withdrew industrial alcohol to the limit of their permits, stored it awhile and then shipped it out to bootleggers who posed as wholesalers, jobbers or fake sales corporations. There were also many forged permits which usually were honored without much investigation. Some of the alcohol was used by the bootleggers without being treated at all, but most of it was sent to "cleaning plants" where an attempt was made to convert it to pure alcohol by redistillation.

Whether the basic ingredient was industrial alcohol, moonshine alcohol or real liquor that had been smuggled into the country, it finally went to what was known as a "cutting plant," where it was mixed with water and flavoring and bottled as imitation whiskey or gin. By the time prohibition was fully under way, there were thousands of such plants, big and small. As with stills, some were little family operations, while others were in large warehouses where crews worked day and night.

Alcohol or a quantity of real whiskey was poured into a vat, warm water was stirred into it, burnt sugar or caramel was added for coloring and oil of rye or bourbon for flavor. If the cutter wanted to make imitation scotch instead of rye or bourbon, he used creosote and a different coloring; if he wanted to mix gin, he used oil of juniper. It was then poured into appropriate bottles, with proper fake labels, packaged to look like the genuine article and delivered to speakeasies or to bootleggers, who peddled it to their customers. Large cutting plants were well protected by payoffs and political influence.

Printers turned out fake labels to match those of every well-known brand. Other suppliers provided trade-marked corks, bottles in distinctive shapes, wrappings similar to those used for genuine liquor and boxes or burlap bags with the names of British or Canadian distillers on them. Brandy, rum, liqueurs and whatever else the customers wanted were produced basically the same way, with the use of various extracts and colorings, warm water and enough raw alcohol to bring it up to proof. The public generally came to realize that most of the liquor was synthetic, but people took what they could get. Most of it had to be drowned with ginger ale or fruit juice to get it down.

The biggest hole in the Volstead Act was the one through which beer freely flowed. Beer was supposed to be outlawed by the Volstead Act, and all breweries were supposed to close down. But it also allowed them to reopen as "cereal beverage" plants, to manufacture what became known as near-beer, which was not to contain more than one-half of one per cent alcohol. Practically nobody wanted to drink near-beer, but before long there were some five hundred breweries given permits to produce it. Nearly all of them pumped out real beer instead.

The cover-up was that near-beer could be made only by first making real beer, in the usual way and at the usual alcoholic strength. By law, the brewery was then supposed to draw off the alcohol until the beer had been reduced to the legal limit of near-beer. The government lacked enough agents to keep a constant check on the breweries, so it was easy enough for most of them merely to switch hoses and fill up barrels with real beer that was shipped out labeled as near-beer.

Since making full-strength beer was part of the legal manufacturing process, prohibition agents could do nothing about it as long as it remained in the brewery. If they suspected that real beer was being shipped out instead of near-beer, they had to capture it in transit, outside the brewery, and then try to prove in court where it had come from. Brewers kept lookouts, to time their shipments when no agents were around, and they also paid protection money to make sure that the law was looking the other way when the trucks rolled out.

The great bulk of good liquor on hand when the nation went dry was held in government-guarded warehouses for medicinal use, to be released to wholesalers who sold it under permit to drugstores to fill doctors' prescriptions. Within months after the start of prohibition, there were more than three thousand wholesalers withdrawing medicinal liquor on permits and some fifty-seven thousand druggists had applied

But Not a Friend of Mine

William Jennings Bryan.

Frances E. Willard.

Carry Nation.   *New York Public Library*

Supporters of prohibition paraded to publicize their cause.
                                 New York Public Library

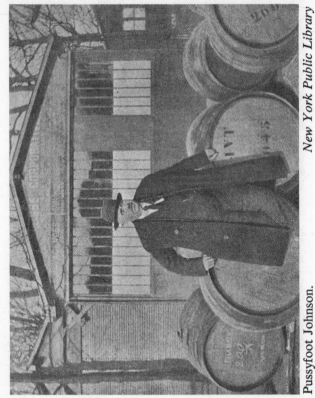

Pussyfoot Johnson.

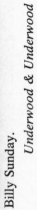

Billy Sunday.

This mock funeral of John Barleycorn was held in Boston when the Prohibition Amendment went into effect.

Underwood & Underwood

Raids on saloons were common in the years before prohibition became the law of the land. *New York Public Library*

Sacks and barrels of corn, sugar and malt were seized in a federal raid on a Chicago brewery linked to gangland boss Al Capone. *New York Public Library*

Speakeasies like this one were commonplace in the 1920s.
The Bettman Archive

The bread lines of the Great Depression brought an end to prohibition.

for permits to buy it. Some wholesale houses were merely fronts for bootleggers, who actually became liquor dealers and seldom carried more than a token line of other drug products. By mixing good liquor with water and alcohol, they could rebottle it and divert half the supply to the illegal trade. Even the remainder that was sold to drugstores often was cut by the retail druggists themselves.

Meanwhile, the number of doctors who obtained permits to write prescriptions for whiskey gradually rose by more than one hundred thousand a year. In theory, each of the eleven million annual whiskey prescriptions they wrote was supposed to be carefully checked, but there were never enough agents to check one prescription in a thousand. Almost anybody who wanted a bottle of whiskey could get a prescription to buy it by paying some doctor a two-dollar office call fee. There were also hundreds of thousands of fake, forged and counterfeit prescriptions circulated all over the country. To get one filled, a customer merely took some doctor's name from the phone book, forged his signature, and presented the blank at the nearest drugstore.

The loophole that let wine pour out was a provision in the Volstead Act that permitted making fruit juices at home and also protected the vinegar industry and let farmers make cider. The maker was supposed to see that it was not allowed to ferment, but there was nothing to stop him from putting it aside to let nature take its course. During prohibition California's grape growers more than doubled their shipments, most of which went to big-city areas, where families supplemented their incomes by producing wine for friends, neighbors and bootleggers.

Desperate drinkers who couldn't afford bootleg liquor or who failed to find a ready source turned to drinking perfume, hair tonic, bay rum, the drainings of farm silos, radiator anti-freeze and canned heat. Such alcoholic products gave many drinkers splitting headaches, knocked them cold, left them with stomach troubles, blinded or killed them. There also were all kinds of patent medicines, low in medicinal value but high in alcoholic content. Probably the worst was a fluid extract of Jamaica ginger, popularly known as "Jake." Even small amounts could cause a terrible form of muscular paralysis that claimed at least fifteen thousand victims, some of whom never fully regained the use of their hands and feet.

Americans by the thousands made their own liquor, beer and wine. There were magazine articles and many books that told them how to distill alcohol in tea kettles, coffee pots, washbasins and other household utensils. Anybody who wanted to make larger quantities at home could buy a hundred pounds of sugar corn for five dollars and a portable one-gallon still for seven dollars more. Prohibition authorities warned that it was illegal to use such equipment, but nobody paid much attention. Amateur distillers began using everything from apples, oats, barley, beets, berries, peaches and apricots to rotted cactus to make liquor. Stores sprang up by the hundreds to sell all the supplies and apparatus the home distiller or brewer might need.

Many citizens preferred to buy their alcohol from bootleggers and then mix their own liquor by adding water and flavorings. Sometimes the family bathtub was filled with water and alcohol, and juniper drops were added to produce what became known as "bathtub gin." There were scores of different flavorings on the market, so that a splash of this or that would produce imitation rye, bourbon, scotch or whatever the amateur mix-master and his guests desired. Matching skills at home distilling and brewing became a popular indoor sport.

Once the knowledge of how to make liquor, beer and wine at home became widespread, there was nothing that could stop the flood. The springs of illegal liquor rose in homes in nearly every neighborhood. Production had become so decentralized that the hope of drying up all the sources of liquor became totally impossible. Millions of Americans were breaking the law, and there was no force on earth big enough to spread out into each home and stop them. With a good part of the public eager to do business with bootleggers, the commercial traffic also flourished. Liquor poured across the land—if not freely, at least liberally.

Meanwhile, a small band of men, whether they liked it or not, had been given the impossible task of trying to hold back the invasion of liquor smugglers at the nation's seacoast and land borders. The federal defenders of a dry America included undermanned and poorly equipped units of several government agencies, spread out so thinly that their total force averaged only about one man for each twelve miles.

11

The self-styled "King of Rum Runners," Bill McCoy, set the pattern for the smuggling of liquor by sea. He was a Florida boatyard operator at the start of prohibition and among the first to realize that the demand for liquor would turn the neighboring British Bahamas into a primary supply source for the bootleg trade.

From the profits he made from an initial run of fifteen hundred cases of whiskey from the Bahamas to Georgia, he was able to buy a schooner he named the *Tomoka*, the first of a fleet of rum ships he operated. Late in May, 1921, he loaded aboard a cargo of liquor in Nassau and sailed it north to anchor off the Long Island coast, beyond what was then the three-mile limit. Bootleggers were tipped off that he was coming, and they sent dozens of small boats out from the Long Island shore to take aboard cases of liquor from the *Tomoka* at sea. Within hours, the entire cargo was sold and the pattern for what was to become Rum Row was established.

McCoy himself made a voyage a month, successfully dodging the Coast Guard for three years, and in that time delivered an estimated three million dollars' worth of illegal liquor. He always insisted that since his was a British ship and since he didn't enter American waters, he wasn't breaking any law. He made pals of writers and newsmen who glamorized him as a romantic outlaw of the sea, claimed he would never stand for gangland violence and once rescued a Treasury agent from a beating by bootleggers.

The Coast Guard cutter *Seneca* chased down McCoy's *Tomoka* off the New Jersey shore late in 1923. When agents boarded the schooner after a wild fist-fight with the crew, McCoy ordered the vessel to sail with the federal agents still aboard. He threatened to kidnap them and carry them back to Nassau, where British courts would have jurisdiction. After a running battle in which the Coast Guard cutter fired warning shots at the *Tomoka*, McCoy was convinced that if he tried to kidnap the agents the government might order the whole Navy to pursue him, and he surrendered. Indicted by a federal grand jury, he remained free on bail for two years while his case dragged through the courts. He finally spent nine months in prison. By the end of that time, the bootleg syndicates had taken over the smuggling racket, so he sold out his interests and lived comfortably in Florida until his death in 1948.

But the pattern McCoy had set grew into a "ghost flotilla" of hundreds of other rum ships. So many rum-runners followed in the wake of McCoy's *Tomoka* that there was hardly a section of the coast without "mother" ships waiting offshore with liquor to supply bootleggers who came out to them in everything from rafts and rowboats to tugs and cabin cruisers.

The most notorious Rum Row was concentrated off Long Island and the New Jersey shore, with sometimes as many as one hundred ships just beyond the three-mile limit. Others anchored off Savannah, Norfolk, Baltimore and Boston. There was a group of ships off Florida and another that operated in the Gulf of Mexico, and Pacific Coast smugglers soon copied the Eastern system with supply ships that ran liquor down from Vancouver and up from Mexico.

One thing the rum-runners seldom carried was rum. The name was a romantic holdover from the rum smuggling of colonial days and from the habit of referring to all liquor as the "demon rum." Most of their cargo was whiskey, legally imported into the British Bahamas and other ports in the West Indies and Central America, and taken aboard by the rum-runners there. Before prohibition came to the United States, the Bahamas had imported only about fifty thousand quarts of whiskey a year, but within two years its imports had soared to more than ten million quarts.

Nassau was transformed from a quiet tropical village to a wide-open boom town, swarming with fat-walleted liquor buyers from the United States and with their thugs and gunmen. There were fights, knifings and shootings. Up off Newfoundland the French islands of St. Pierre and Miquelon provided the rum-runners with another safe port close to the mainland, and shared on a smaller scale in the prosperity and problems brought by the liquor trade.

Both the rum-runners and the seagoing bootleggers were far less worried over being captured by the undermanned federal forces than by the possibility that they might be robbed or murdered by hijacking pirates who ranged up and down the coast. Most rum ships were well armed to fight off hijackers, and there were frequent battles at sea. But the smaller craft were the main prey of the gangsters who roamed Rum Row in fast boats to rob anybody they could catch and overpower. Bootleggers carried large sums of money to pay for liquor, and the pirates jumped them on their way out to the rum ships. Such attacks often went unreported until days later, when the bodies of men who had been shot and thrown overboard drifted to shore.

After long negotiations the United States won an agreement with Britain and other foreign nations to extend territorial waters. This pushed Rum Row about twelve miles out to sea and just about put an end to the ship-to-shore bootlegging by small craft and the pirates who preyed upon them. But forcing most of the smaller bootleggers out of business also strengthened the control of the big bootlegging syndicates. They equipped themselves with larger and faster boats for the runs from shore and soon organized the entire sea smuggling racket.

The rum ships they owned and chartered still served as offshore supply stations, but instead of being met by any little bootlegger who sent a small boat from shore they were visited at night by high-powered speedboats that were specially designed and equipped to outrun anything the Coast Guard could put into the water. Supply ships were shifted about, and their movements, as well as those of the speedboats, were directed by illegal short-wave radio stations, which gave them coded instructions and information about landing areas. Some syndicates used seaplanes to help direct the fast-moving operations and to warn of the approach of Coast Guard cutters.

Illegal radio stations put out fake S.O.S. calls to draw Coast Guard cutters away from unloading rum ships and to send them racing to the rescue of some imaginary vessel in distress. Sometimes old ships were deliberately set afire and then abandoned by their crews to distract the Coast Guard. Empty rum ships acted as decoys to lead the Coast Guard into chasing them into areas far from actual operations, and their crews often spiced the chase by tossing empty liquor cases overboard so that pursuing Coast Guard men would think they were closing in on the real quarry. Ship flags and markings were doctored so rum boats would look like other vessels.

Many chases were spectacular and dangerous, with the open firing of guns and races for miles as they circled through fog and rough seas and skirted hidden reefs and sandbars. Some cutters were led, with guns roaring, right into New York Harbor. One Coast Guard cutter pursued two speedboats along the Coney Island beach on a hot July day, so close to shore that a mob of bathers were thrown into near-panic. Excited Coney Island police rushed out to a pier and began firing their pistols at the bootleggers, who waved to them and kept on going. Before long, the Coast Guard had lost eight men, killed in action in various chases, and eighteen gansters had been killed or wounded. Scores of speedboats were seized, but hundreds more escaped.

When prohibition started, the Coast Guard was a small arm of the Treasury Department, concerned with the protection of government revenues and the prevention of ordinary smuggling, but also with its major peacetime duty of saving lives and property at sea. It had only a few hundred officers, a few thousand enlisted men, about thirty cutters and a number of small harbor boats and launches. Because of prohibition the Coast Guard was greatly expanded, until it gradually became one of the full military services of the United States, although still the smallest. Limited funds were appropriated at first, but they finally grew to many millions of dollars, and the service was given more officers, men and vessels, including a small fleet of inactive destroyers transferred from the Navy.

Fighting the flow of liquor from the sea became its major job until at the peak of its strength in prohibition years the Coast Guard had some three hundred destroyers, cutters and large patrol boats—but spread along the coasts that meant only one vessel to cover every three hundred square miles of water within the twelve-mile limit. During its fourteen years of rum warfare the Coast Guard seized thousands of bootlegging boats, cut profits of the bootleggers and made their smuggling more difficult. But until the end, the gangsters who smuggled by sea so greatly outnumbered the Coast Guard over such enormous distances that it could never more than slow them down.

Federal agents along the land borders and lake and river boundaries were even less successful. Two years after America went dry, the Prohibition Bureau admitted that it probably was keeping only one case of liquor in twenty from entering the country. Canada's distilleries and breweries provided an almost unlimited source of whiskey and beer for American bootleg syndicates. In addition, imports of British liquor into Canada increased eight times in the prohibition years. Mexico also produced and shipped large quantities.

Trucks and touring cars loaded with whiskey could be pointed toward some four hundred different roads and at least one hundred known trails that led into the United States from Canada. Liquor could be run by speedboat by way of the Great Lakes and the Detroit and St. Lawrence Rivers. Up from Mexico there were at least two hundred possible roads and trails, as well as many shallow crossings offered by the Rio Grande. During prohibition's first years there were not more than one hundred prohibition agents assigned to the Canadian border and only thirty-five to watch the Mexican border.

American bootleggers operating out of Canada and Mexico smuggled liquor not only in trucks but often by the carload, aboard freight trains. Whiskey would be hidden in loads of other goods and mixed with legitimate freight, in boxes supposed to contain fish, fruit or hardware. Inspection frequently was brief and routine, since legitimate freight might be perishable and couldn't be unduly delayed. Sometimes bribes were paid and stolen and counterfeit customs seals were used. Smugglers also frequently used airplanes, some of which operated on regular flight schedules.

Small-time bootleggers packed liquor on their backs and walked across the border at remote spots, or carried a few cases on horses or mules. Some floated barrels across shallow waterways. There were those who went through regular customs checkpoints wheeling baby carriages that held a case of liquor beneath a squawling infant, others who wore suits designed with many pockets to hold concealed pints of whiskey, some who wrapped liquor-filled garden hoses around their bodies under their clothing and women who hid liquor under their skirts.

Few thirsty American tourists came back without a bottle or two. What each could carry wasn't much, but it added up when multiplied by the more than one million Americans who flocked to Canada every year. Prohibition also made small smugglers of many transatlantic travelers and of sailors who stole whiskey from their ships and peddled it to waterfront speakeasies.

But although the borders were penetrated at almost every mile by every sort of smuggling attempt, the greatest quantity of liquor came across rivers and lakes from Canada aboard fast boats. Some carried only four or five cases. Others were speedy and well-equipped rum cutters that could haul up to a thousand cases at a crossing. To make a rich profit, they had to land only about one load out of five, and their average was far better than that. Federal officials estimated that there were at least fifteen hundred liquor boats operating between Canada and the United States within five years after the start of prohibition. Many raced across the water boundaries to isolated docks and beaches on the American side, where trucks were waiting to haul the liquor to city cutting plants.

They ran across the St. Lawrence to small towns in upper New York, across the Niagara River to Buffalo, through the Great Lakes to Duluth, Toledo, Cleveland, Sandusky, Erie and other ports, and down Lake Champlain to places in New York and Vermont. But the busiest traffic was across the Detroit River. More liquor was landed at Detroit docks than at all other border cities combined. Under the control of the syndicates, and with political and police protection, the bootleggers for a time made Detroit the principal port of entry for liquor smuggled into the United States.

"At least $35,000,000 worth of liquor comes to Detroit annually through a hugh funnelneck—the 70 miles of river and lakefront stretching from the village of St. Clair to South Rockwood," the *Detroit News* reported in 1928. "On the Canadian side of the waterway lie the liquor docks of the exporters, drawing their stores from a potential source of 83 breweries and 23 distilleries . . ."

Gangsters were said to be paying two million dollars in graft in Detroit alone. Everywhere in the United States prohibition was feeding power and money to the gangs that took control of the liquor which had been put outside the law.

12

By the time Warren Harding had been president for only little more than a year, prohibition enforcement had become so blundering that he felt it necessary to call the attention of congress to conditions "which savor of a nation-wide scandal." His successor, Calvin Coolidge, also demanded better enforcement but, like Harding, passed the problems along to congress. Both presidents recommended enforcement funds millions of dollars short of what was needed. Congress, in turn, did hardly anything to solve the real problems of enforcement.

The nation was economy-minded, the drys had promised enforcement would be cheap and politicians had no desire to ask tax-paying voters for more money. The Prohibition Bureau started with an annual budget of less than five million dollars, which was doubled within five years, but by that time the illegal bootlegging trade had become a three billion dollar racket. Bootleg syndicates were better financed, better manned and better organized than those who sought to put them out of business. Hampered by a lack of funds, ruled by politicians and lobbyists, burdened with inefficiency and corruption, prohibition's enforcers could make only a token effort. Total enforcement became a pretense, and evasion of the law became the fact.

Dominated by a dry majority and lulled by dry propaganda that prohibition was a success, congress did little more than echo the platitudes of the dry leaders. Members of the House and Senate rejected nearly all proposals to investigate enforcement, to change the setup or to remove it from the crippling political influence that congress itself wielded. As a result, the Prohibition Bureau served the spoils system and became a pork barrel for the politicians. Jobs as agents were doled out as favors by congressmen or their state patronage bosses. The Anti-Saloon League also passed on applicants, and the League as well as the politicians dictated the decisions of the Bureau.

Throughout prohibition, agents quit their jobs faster than they could be replaced. In one year alone some ten thousand men were hired to keep two thousand jobs filled. The Bureau's difficulty in keeping good men extended to its highest levels. Some states had new prohibition directors every few months. One after another, new national enforcement chiefs took over with the promise of sweeping reforms that ended in frustration.

John F. Kramer, an Ohio lawyer, ardent prohibitionist and old friend of the Anti-Saloon League, entered office as the first Prohibition Commissioner with the announced belief that it was the will of the American people to see the nation become bone-dry and that therefore his task would be easy. By the end of the first year, Kramer admitted that public hostility had created difficult problems and that prohibition had been "to some extent forced upon whole states and especially upon large cities in which people had no sympathy whatever with the idea." Six months after that, he gave up the job.

His successor, Roy Haynes, another Ohioan, a prominent Methodist churchman and long-time supporter of the Anti-Saloon League, was hand-picked for the job by the League's Wayne Wheeler. Haynes worked closely with him to promote the League's policies, and Wheeler used his influence to keep Haynes in office. The charge was frequently made that Wheeler, working through Haynes, was the real boss of dry enforcement in the United States.

Within two years, Haynes was claiming that he had the illegal liquor traffic under control and that enforcement was "rapidly approaching the highest point of its efficiency." He declared that "the home brew fad is taking its final gasp," that "bootleg patronage has fallen off fifty per cent," that "moonshining in the cities is on the wane" and that millions of Americans had stopped drinking. By 1923 he was ready to assert that the bootlegging business had "reached a desperate plight," and that "its death rattle has begun" and "there is but little open and aboveboard drinking anywhere."

The obvious facts seemed to contradict his wishful statistics. Political appointments had filled the Prohibition Bureau with incompetents. Graft and corruption had spread. Bootlegging had become gang-controlled and had grown to a major industry. Despite Haynes's best efforts and his statements to the contrary, violation of the prohibition laws had become an American way of life.

The truth was so apparent by 1925 that President Coolidge decided to put a military man, retired General Lincoln C. Andrews, in charge of enforcement. Haynes kept his title as Prohibition Commissioner and stayed on the government payroll, mainly as a contact man for the politically potent Anti-Saloon League, but Andrews was given the real authority as Assistant Secretary of the Treasury. He made a valiant effort to reorganize enforcement and to drive out the political spoilsmen. For the first time, the Prohibition Bureau, Coast Guard, Customs and other agencies dealing with liquor were brought under unified control. Andrews reorganized the enforcement districts without regard to state lines, brought in retired Army and Navy men, set up mobile squads and shifted personnel so bootleggers would find bribery more difficult.

But when Andrews announced that he intended to purge the Prohibition Bureau by terminating all jobs and reappointing men strictly on the basis of qualifications and merit, the politicians went to work on him. They scuttled Andrews' plans and his program, kept most of their politically appointed men from being dismissed and forced him to back down. Many of his supporters were hounded out of the service, and others were transferred to positions of little influence. Before long, most of the reorganization existed only on paper, and corruption and graft went on as usual.

Andrews resigned in March, 1927, and was succeeded by Assistant Secretary of the Treasury Seymour Lowman. When Haynes finally left the government payroll a former chief chemist of the Prohibition Bureau, James M. Doran, was named Commissioner. But it wasn't until 1930 that a really stable enforcement agency began to take command, and by then it was far too late.

Like congress and the presidents, state officials talked a lot about prohibition but did little about the real problems of enforcement. The states kept dry voters and lobbyists happy by passing plenty of enforcement laws, but they put neither money nor manpower behind them. Despite constant pleas from Washington for more help, the states actually gave the federal government hardly anything but verbal support.

Many state and city laws were far more drastic than the federal law, but enforcement was something else. On the average, the states spent four times as much to maintain parks and monuments as to enforce prohibition.

Most states put the burden of convictions on federal courts and attorneys and generally let the federal Prohibition Bureau try to cope with violations, with the result that the entire federal court system was all but overwhelmed. Federal attorneys were spending three-fourths of all their time on liquor violations. In five years the unfinished cases on court dockets increased one thousand per cent. Enough arrests were being made in a month to occupy all available federal judges for a year, and there were estimates that in ten years the courts would be a century behind in their work.

Some judges and juries were reluctant to impose harsh penalties. In wet states especially, as the Prohibition Bureau reported in 1925, it was "very difficult to get a verdict of any consequence." Faced with public hostility in the very areas where the court jams were the greatest, the federal government began to establish "bargain days" and "cafeteria courts," where justice was dispensed with a broad hand that required no jury trials. On certain days set aside on the court calendar, swarms of bootleggers, speakeasy proprietors, moonshiners, smugglers and others accused of violating the law entered quick guilty pleas after being assured in advance that if they cooperated they would escape jail sentences. Fines averaged as little as five or ten dollars, and seldom exceeded one hundred dollars. The result was what amounted to a system of illegal licensing. Many violators paid less in fines to carry on their business than they had paid in license fees when liquor was legal. They simply went into court, paid the fine and went on bootlegging as usual.

Many raided speakeasies were back in business almost as soon as the raiders left and the Prohibition Bureau, looking for a way to make its raids more effective and still not overload the courts, began to padlock raided places. The Volstead Act provided that a place where liquor was sold or kept could be padlocked as "a common nuisance" by a simple court injunction and for a time it was the most effective method the government had to enforce prohibition. In New York, five hundred speakeasies were padlocked in a single year, and hundreds were shut in other cities. Some large hotels were among the places padlocked, and zealous raiders festooned one illegal distillery with two hundred padlocks to make sure all its vats were shut down.

Some prohibition agents were accused of going too far by padlocking the front doors of private homes where it was suspected that liquor was being made. In Northern California, agents even padlocked a big redwood tree that had been hollowed out to conceal a fifty-gallon still operated by moonshiners. The federal men looped a chain around it, snapped a padlock, and hung a sign on the tree that read: "Closed for one year for violation of the National Prohibition Act."

But there weren't enough agents to keep a check on places that had been padlocked. Locks were picked, broken open or evaded. Lawyers for the bootleg syndicates learned to create so many legal technicalities that agents had trouble getting court injunctions. Gradually padlocking was abandoned for other methods.

Whatever they tried, with never enough men or money, the enforcers couldn't hope to catch more than a small percentage of those who violated the prohibition laws, and few of those they did catch were severely punished. Enforcement fell into a hit-and-miss pattern, carried out in sporadic raids that concentrated on one area or one type of violation while others had to be ignored. A forceful crusade or flurry of arrests would be followed by a return to the conditions that had existed before. Federal agents across the country, as well as local police in some areas, made thousands of small raids on speakeasies, hotels, amusement parks, pool halls, fruit stands and delicatessens. They carried them out with great energy and ingenuity and sometimes at the risk of their lives. But the basic problems remained, and the raids seldom amounted to more than a passing annoyance to the organized bootleg syndicates.

Probably the most publicized of federal agents were the New York team of Izzy Einstein and Moe Smith, who between them made more than four thousand arrests and confiscated more than fifteen million dollars' worth of liquor in four years. Their colorful and often comic adventures as heroes of the enforcement service kept newspaper and magazine readers highly entertained.

Izzy and Moe adopted all sorts of disguises to pursue the trail of illegal liquor. They posed as automobile mechanics, opera singers, band musicians, milk wagon drivers, grave diggers, pushcart vendors, fishermen, longshoremen, horse dealers, streetcar conductors, lawyers, football players, Polish counts, seedy pawnshop patrons and Broadway actors. They perspiringly marched in a Fourth of July parade to gain information that led to raids, took over an ice wagon route that made deliveries to Brooklyn saloons and pretended to be meat salesmen offering speakeasies turkeys for Thanksgiving banquets. Izzy once sang as a soloist at a German beer garden, and when he had accepted applause for his number, announced, "That concludes the evening's entertainment. This place is pinched."

Their high score was seventeen raids in a single night, but for a considerable time they shut down an average of twenty places a week. Although they won high praise from dry leaders, some Washington officials of the Prohibition Bureau became jealous of their personal publicity. Others disliked the fact that their clowning exploits kept the nation laughing at what was the serious business of law enforcement. Their activities pointed up the fact that the government, unable to halt the major sources of supply, was forced to resort to such detective methods in a never-ending series of small attempts to dry up liquor almost drop by drop. Both men finally left the service and became successful life insurance salesmen.

But if people laughed at Izzy and Moe and regarded their chase of the bootleggers as good sport, there was less public laughter over some of the other activities of prohibition enforcers. Many protested against their snooping into private lives, using wire-tapping and informers, bribing witnesses, and employing various entrapment tricks that enticed people to break the law so they could be caught. There was an uproar when it was revealed that the federal government had gone into the business of operating a speakeasy in a fashionable section of Manhattan and had shared in the management of other drinking places for liquor spying purposes. Public opinion was even more outraged over the increasing number of people who died or who became seriously ill from drinking denatured alcohol. Some critics charged that by deliberately doctoring industrial alcohol with deadly poisons the government was responsible for the "brutal murder" of its own citizens.

But, more than anything else, the nation was shocked by the violence and corruption that grew out of prohibition enforcement. By 1931, sixty federal agents had lost their lives in gun battles and the federal men had killed about three times that many civilians. There were many more shootings by state agents, constables, police, special officers and other enforcers over whom the federal government had no control. While the federal men usually used their guns only in self-defense or with justifiable reason, overzealous local lawmen often fired with less caution.

Civilians were killed by officers who invaded their property without warrants, were shot down on lonely roads when they became frightened and tried to escape from officers who wore no uniforms to identify them and were killed by stray bullets during gun chases. Maryland's Senator Millard Tydings estimated that during the first ten years of prohibition 1,365 people were killed in attempts to enforce the law, and the *Washington Herald*, after a nationwide survey, came up with almost the same estimate and added that at least one thousand others had been wounded.

Bribery and payoffs became so common that they were taken for granted. Everybody knew that bootleg syndicates and speakeasies couldn't operate without putting police, sheriffs and other officials on their payrolls. There was hardly any state, county or large city where charges were not brought at one time or another that officials were working with the liquor gangs. Hundreds of judges, prosecuting attorneys, mayors, aldermen, heads of city departments, county officers, state legislators, police chiefs and other supposed upholders of law and order were indicted over the years, sometimes in wholesale lots that included an entire city or county administration.

Among the federal enforcement agencies, none escaped the corruption of bootleg bribes. Investigations revealed that low-salaried Prohibition Bureau agents were buying country homes, town houses, expensive cars, furs and jewelry. Some were so carelessly affluent that they reported for work in chauffeur-driven cars. There were charges that many agents stayed on the job only long enough to learn the ropes and make the necessary contacts, and then quit to become bootleggers or speakeasy operators themselves.

Customs agents and Treasury men also frequently were charged with taking bribes or conspiring to help liquor smugglers, and even the Coast Guard, probably the cleanest of the federal agencies helping to enforce prohibition, had whole crews of men and officers accused of corruption.

Evading and mocking the Volstead Act became sort of a "national sport" as the booming prosperity that roared in with the Twenties changed the American way of life. It was the age of the automobile, the movies, the radio, of new excitements, new freedoms and easy living, and the spirit of the age was to take nothing seriously except making money and having fun.

Middle-class Americans had been the strongest supporters of prohibition, but as they became the richest middle class in the world many wanted to imitate the fads and fashions of the wealthy. The moralizing reformers of the past were ridiculed as "bluenoses" who were trying to spoil the fun, and the cocktail shaker became a symbol of revolt. In many homes where liquor seldom had been served, drinking became the socially "smart" thing to do; when the middle class took to drinking publicly in great numbers, prohibition lost its main support.

Women, who had never joined their men in much public drinking, flocked to the bars as soon as liquor was made illegal, with what seemed to be the same show of rebellion that made them bob their hair and shorten their skirts to gain freedom from the old-fashioned ways. They shocked some of their elders, as they probably intended, and especially alarmed the drys, who had always argued that one of the main reasons for prohibition was to protect women from the evils of the saloon. But feminine drinking soon became customary.

Mothers and fathers who drank had a hard time convincing sons and daughters that only parents should evade prohibition. Youth also rebelled; for some young people, drinking forbidden liquor was an act of bravado that seemed romantic and adventurous. In some cities and well-to-do suburban areas there were speakeasies that catered to the high school set, while Joe College often tried to match his father's home skill by making his own gin in dormitory bathtubs. There were plenty of bootleggers near most college campuses to keep the pockets of racoon coats well supplied with pint bottles and to fill the garter-held flasks of flappers.

The hip flask, so often pictured in popular cartoons of the day, turned every parking place and wooded lane into a portable bar. But the flask was not solely the possession of the young. Some men and women used flasks to carry liquor wherever they went and also carried it in hollow canes, briefcases and thermos bottles. In many offices where the serving of "a quick one" became a routine of business life, bottles were concealed in hidden desk bars and behind false-fronted rows of shelved books. Home liquor cabinets also were often elaborately tricked out for concealment to add to the spice of the national pastime of turning the Volstead Act into a game of Hide and Seek.

Bootleggers were everywhere and of all kinds. In prohibition's early days some bootleggers were amateurs who supplied liquor to their friends as a source of part-time income. Bootlegging also became a profitable sideline for some housewives, and until the gangsters organized the business a host of small-time bootleggers competed for trade. In some areas, there were so many that they engaged in price-cutting wars. Business cards, price lists and circulars were freely distributed. In most cities, a phone call to the neighboring bootlegger would bring immediate home delivery.

The bootlegger's car, often a long and sleek black sedan, became so familiar on its weekend rounds of residential streets that it seldom attracted more attention than the milk wagon. Some estimates put the national total of bootleggers as high as one million, but there were too many part-timers to make any figure more than a guess. A newspaper survey counted five thousand professional bootleggers in the city of Washington alone. Visitors to White House functions during President Harding's administration found liquor readily available in the upstairs hall, and federal enforcement officials publicly complained that "bootleggers infest the halls and corridors of congress."

Aside from bootleggers, city suppliers of bottled liquor included taxi drivers, hotel bellhops, shoeshine boys, barbers, druggists, clerks at soda fountains, fruit juice stands and cigar stores and operators of delicatessens, paint stores, groceries, garages, laundries and express offices. The *New York Telegram* in 1929 listed nearly one hundred types of establishments where liquor could be bought, including boardinghouses, political and social clubs, gymnasiums and dancing academies. Some large office buildings had bootleggers whose entire trade was within the one building.

Like the saloons they replaced, speakeasies were of every variety, but there were a lot more of them than there ever had been saloons. In New York City alone, police estimated in 1929 that there were thirty-two thousand speakeasies and admitted the count was far from complete. Some were back-alley joints where the rawest liquor sold for a dime a drink, and others were expensively decorated lounges with subdued lighting and excellent service where a cocktail might cost a dollar and a half. As New York Police Commissioner Grover Whalen said, "All you need is two bottles and a room and you have a speakeasy."

Across the country, they operated in back rooms, basements and first-floor flats, sometimes with so many in a neighborhood that other residents put up a sign, "This is no speakeasy." Most of them were behind plain doors that were locked and provided with peepholes, so the customer had to go through a ritual of showing an "honorary" membership card or otherwise identifying himself as eligible to join the company of happy law-breakers. "Joe sent me," became a popular password of the times.

There were few secrets that the speakeasy had to hide from the police and federal agents who usually were well paid to see that nothing interfered with business, but the peephole ritual added to the atmosphere and helped convince the customer that he was someone special who was permitted to enter an exclusive club. Getting into a speakeasy was considered part of the fun. Some places dressed up their operations by providing hidden entrances through phone booths or secret doors from cigar stores, garages and dental offices. One popular speakeasy in a New Jersey suburb was behind the vault of a savings bank. But many operated quite openly, even if forced away from the street corners where the old swinging-door saloons had been. There were no legal closing hours, age limits or other restrictions, and the behavior of patrons depended on what rules the bartender wanted to enforce.

Expenses were high. Landlords charged speakeasies up to three times the normal rent. A city speakeasy might have to pay five hundred dollars a month in protection money to police and prohibition agents, as well as graft to the district attorney's office, other politicians and fire and health department inspectors, and fifty dollars to the cop on the beat every time a beer delivery was made. Added to that were the threats of robbery, shooting or bombing by a rival, blackmail, extortion, the cutting off of sources of supply and raids that couldn't be prevented, or a padlocking that might wipe out the operator's total investment. When public opinion demanded a show of enforcement for the sake of the record, speakeasy proprietors sometimes were tipped off in advance so they could put away their expensive stock and leave a few cheap bottles out for the expected raiders to seize and smash. In some cities, when a place was raided there would be a rebate of protection money in the amount of whatever fines or court costs had to be paid before business could be resumed.

Speakeasies flourished while the boom of the Twenties lasted and almost everybody had plenty of money to spend, but the depression brought them hard times and thousands were forced out of business. Some that survived began to cut prices to lure people away from their homes, where the middle class found it cheaper to drink during prohibition's last years. By then most of the independent speakeasy operators had long departed from the scene, having given up for lack of profit or in fear of their lives to the criminal syndicates that took over the better locations.

Most of the nightclubs of the Twenties, in New York and other big cities, were dominated by gangsters. Dedicated to the business of devising as many ways as possible to part a fool from his money, they provided a gaudy showcase for socialites, who got a thrill from mingling with underworld characters, and for so-called big spenders, whose idea of fun was to get as drunk and as loud as they could. Prices were high, the food was terrible and the entertainment brash and boisterous. There were excessive cover charges, minimum charges and often deliberate mistakes in adding up bills, and in some of the real clip joints drinks were drugged so that anything still remaining in a patron's wallet could be extracted. In the "better" places the process of robbery was more genteel, and most victims were willing and often eager to surrender their cash to fortify their egos.

Texas Guinan, the queen of New York's prohibition nightclubs, greeted her customers with the cheery shout, "Hello, suckers," and they loved it. Born on a ranch in Waco,

Texas, Mary Louise Cecilia Guinan hoped for a musical career, but joined a circus as a bronco rider instead. She went into vaudeville, drifted to Hollywood, where she played parts in Western movies, and then came to Broadway to act in a musical comedy. She wasn't much of a success as a singer or dancer, but she made an immediate hit in nightclubs as a mistress of ceremonies.

A brassy-voiced, wisecracking blonde whose personality seemed to typify the spirit of the Roaring Twenties, she was discovered by horse-faced racketeer Larry Fay, who starred her in half a dozen of the clubs he operated. Sponsored by Fay and other gangsters, she opened a successive number of Texas Guinan Clubs, starting up a new one every time an old one was shut by prohibition raiders. Always ready to romp with the customers and keep things moving at a fast pace, she and her various partners took in thousands of dollars a week, although when she died in 1933 at the age of forty-nine, Texas Guinan had little of it left.

One night, when a wealthy drunk at one of her clubs began handing out fifty-dollar bills to everybody in sight, she dragged him up to the microphone and jokingly introduced him as "a big butter-and-egg man," and for a time the phrase became part of the nation's speech as a slang term for a sporty big spender. Another expression she used became familiar with masters of ceremonies everywhere. When one of her showgirls finished performing, she would lead the applause with the shout, "Give this little girl a great big hand!" The only time Texas Guinan was topped was when a federal agent, during a raid, caught her arm and called out to his men, "Give this little girl a great big handcuff!"

Her places were frequently raided, but she turned most of the raids into a joke. When the federal men broke in to haul her off to court, she sometimes had the band strike up "The Prisoner's Song." Half a dozen Texas Guinan Clubs were padlocked and she was arrested many times, but she never went to jail and seldom was detained in court more than a few hours. Fines were paid or the proper political strings were pulled, and she was back entertaining again—if not at the old stand, then at a new one. She wore a necklace strung with small gold padlocks, like service stripes, and one of her diamond bracelets had a tiny police whistle on it for a good-luck charm.

Larry Fay, who promoted her to stardom, started as a small-time hoodlum who gained control of a fleet of taxicabs, some of which were used to smuggle liquor from Canada at the start of prohibition. He became a big-shot rum-runner and racketeer, the first of New York's ruling gangsters to devote himself mainly to night clubs. A vain and far from handsome little man, he spent a fortune on flashy clothes, including specially tailored bulletproof vests. But he forgot to wear one on the day he was shot to death in front of one of his clubs.

There was hardly any leader of New York's underworld who didn't invest in nightclubs at one time or another. They muscled in on already established places and, if they couldn't buy them out, terrorized or murdered the owners. For most of the big criminals, nightclubs were a sideline to smuggling, bootlegging, brewing and distilling and all the associated crimes supported by the flood of money from the liquor rackets. Murder became the accepted gangland method of eliminating competition. Gang warfare began when greedy mobsters invaded each other's territories. Although shootings in Chicago and some other cities gained greater publicity, there were more than one thousand gang killings in New York during the prohibition years.

Long before the Eighteenth Amendment was enacted criminal gangs had risen to power in many cities, partly through control of the old-time saloons. But while prohibition did not create organized crime, it did create an enormous new area of criminal opportunity that offered less risk and more certain profit than older fields of crime, and produced a general public indifference that lawbreakers had never enjoyed before. It provided a steady income of millions of dollars that let criminals expand their forces and gain power of control over whole cities and states. Prohibition supplied the "golden grease" for the interlocking machinery of crime, politics, courts and police, which won protection not only for the liquor rackets but also for the spread of all other criminal activities.

Almost with immunity from the law, gangsters moved into high places of government, into legitimate business, labor unions, employers' associations, industrial racketeering, the protection rackets, blackmail and extortion. They also stepped up older forms of crime, such as vice, crooked gambling, robbery, larceny, kidnaping and killing for hire. Gang bosses supplied hoodlums to help unions enforce strikes and also to help companies smash unions. They looted public services and private corporations, and bought their way into the manipulation of stocks, real estate and concerns manufacturing all sorts of products from sporting goods to slot machines.

Prohibition fixed upon the United States a pattern of organized crime that was to go on for years. But in the Twenties, it was in Chicago that the gangs reached almost incredible power.

13

Big Jim Colosimo was the king of Chicago's underworld when prohibition came, and he hired a New York thug, Johnny Torrio, as his bodyguard and general assistant. Torrio, a smart operator who soon started to move in on his boss, saw prohibition as a golden opportunity, but Colosimo apparently didn't agree and insisted that they should stick to the rackets they had. In May, 1920, Colosimo was shot to death and Torrio took over. He created Chicago's bootleg empire and masterminded it for five years with such control that the public hardly became aroused.

Torrio's first step was to make a deal with a socially prominent attorney whose family owned five breweries supposedly shut down by prohibition but still in operation. He then tightly sewed up police protection, to the point where he had cops in uniform riding his liquor trucks as guards and could boast, "I own the police." He bought the cooperation of federal prohibition agents and bribed a number of city and state officials by giving them small shares in breweries, speakeasies and gambling joints. With his liquor supply assured and protection guaranteed, he finally called the city's rival gang leaders into conference.

It was senseless and dangerous, Torrio convinced them, to go on fighting each other. If they divided the city into territories of control under his supervision, he could promise them all the beer and liquor they could sell, immunity from interference and a chance for everybody to get rich. Torrio became "board chairman" of the syndicate, kept a good territory for himself, was the wholesale supplier for the other mobsters and mapped out the areas where each of the others would be free to devote full time to developing retail sales outlets and whatever rackets might prove profitable.

As his bodyguard, Torrio brought to Chicago a young gangster recommended by his old pals in New York, a twenty-three-year-old waterfront tough who had a reputation for being as handy with a knife or a blackjack as with a gun. His name was Al Capone. A physically ugly man, with a flat nose, a bull neck and a knife scar that ran from his left ear to his fat lips, Capone seemed determined to prove that his ugliness was not only skin-deep. Within months after he went to work for Torrio in 1920, he had so impressed his new boss that he was put in charge of the Four Deuces Café, an unusual pleasure dome where Torrio maintained his headquarters.

Although he had dropped out of school after the fourth grade, Capone proved an efficient manager of that department store of assorted vices. He also helped Torrio put down a revolt against the syndicate in a series of gang skirmishes in which nine men were killed, and in reward for his various services was chosen by Torrio in 1923 to head the syndicate's expansion into neighboring towns. As Torrio's first lieutenant, Capone spread the territory of gang control and greatly increased its revenues. In suburban Cicero he established his own empire of lucrative crime and came into his own as a top mobster.

Capone opened headquarters at a Cicero inn, where he took over a full floor for his business office, put bulletproof shutters on the windows and posted armed gunmen at each entrance. With the help of his gunmen, who terrorized voters, invaded polling places and seized ballot boxes, he put his handpicked candidates into city offices and became the undisputed ruler of Cicero. His rule was so absolute that one day, when he lost his temper and slugged the mayor, knocking him down the city hall steps, the police politely stood by. Another time, when the city council hesitated about obeying his commands, Capone hoodlums broke into the council chambers, blackjacked one of the councilmen and ordered the others to go home.

Capone transformed Cicero into the wildest city in the country, multiplied its saloons, gambling joints and pleasure resorts and ran them wide open day and night. He made it a protected vacation spot for trigger-happy gangsters who came there from all over the country to relax from the labors of their own criminal operations in other cities, knowing it was one place where police would not annoy them.

By then he was Torrio's full partner, and their combine was operating sixty-five breweries, many distilleries, stills and smaller alcohol cookeries and running large quantities of liquor into Chicago from gang-connected supply sources throughout the Midwest. The combine's net income was estimated at thirty million dollars a year from liquor alone, plus half that much more from other rackets. But one of the Chicago sub-bosses, Dion O'Banion, was giving them trouble. Capone later was quoted as saying that O'Banion's "head got too big for his hat."

O'Banion was a rather handsome man with an exceed-ingly odd personality, a one-time altar boy and singer in a cathedral choir who turned to singing sentimental ballads in tough saloons while learning to become a holdup man, safe-cracker and muscle-man in newspaper circulation wars, and otherwise achieving a long criminal record. When prohibi-tion came, he turned to hijacking and gathered around him some of Chicago's most deadly gunmen. He hijacked Torrio's liquor trucks until Torrio convinced him he could do better by working with the combine and gave O'Banion the richest section of the city as his territory.

Working with the syndicate, O'Banion became one of the wealthier sub-bosses, and among those with the strongest political influence and police protection. Although he had fifty gunmen to do his beatings and killings for him, he apparently liked to keep his hand in by personally taking part in such gang activities. But he also prided himself on being a loving husband and good family man, never missed attending church on Sunday and visited his old slum neighborhood to hand out sums of money to the needy. He took an interest in playing the piano, furnished his home with works of art and indulged his fondest hobby by buying a half-interest in a flower shop, where he spent many hours lovingly arranging floral displays. It was said of him that he not only furnished the wreaths and garlands for the biggest of gangland funerals but also often furnished the corpse.

O'Banion was restless for still more power and took to feuding with Torrio, Capone and others, and got into a price-cutting war that led him to hijack liquor trucks run by an affluent mob known as the Terrible Gennas. The Gennas had five police captains and four hundred patrolmen on their payroll, but that didn't keep O'Banion from making insulting remarks about "them Sicilians" or from quarreling with both

Capone and the Gennas over some unpaid gambling debts. Finally he was suspected of double-crossing Torrio himself by selling him a brewery for half a million dollars and then tipping off police so Torrio would be arrested there during a raid.

He was at his flower shop on a November day in 1924, clipping chrysanthemums intended for an important gangland funeral, when three men arrived to pick up the flowers. O'Banion recognized them and held out his hand to greet them, but they drew revolvers, fired six shots and killed him. Torrio and Capone were briefly questioned by police, along with some of the Terrible Gennas, but there was no proof as to who had ordered O'Banion's execution.

Vowing revenge, the surviving leaders of the O'Banion gang announced that they intended to kill Torrio, Capone, the Gennas and others. Two months later, Torrio was shot in front of his home and seriously wounded. He recovered, but meanwhile the charges that grew out of the brewery double-cross were pressed against him, and he was sent to prison for nine months. While he was behind bars, the bootleg empire he had so carefully built erupted in a full-scale war that eventually involved every gang leader in Chicago. Capone fought Torrio's rivals to try to keep control of the vast organization.

The war went on for five years, with the streets of Chicago as a gangland battleground. Rival mobs openly fired on each other, hurled bombs and hijacked trucks. Even the police tried to work out armistice agreements to get them to respect each other's territories again, but to no avail. Five hundred mobsters were killed, including many of the big shots of crime. Capone kept his place at the top and emerged from the gang wars as the super-boss, but he was never able to bring real peace to the combine or to avoid uprisings and shootings that threatened his position, and his reign was one of constant violence that centered public attention on gangland activities.

Torrio decided to quit. When he came out of prison, after having been shot at and knowing that he was still high on the execution list, he reportedly told Capone, "It's all yours, Al." He turned over to Capone what was a business grossing some seventy million dollars a year and retired to a luxurious seaside villa in Italy, taking with him enough money to keep him in comfort the rest of his life. He later made trips back to the United States, but kept clear of any further gang operations in Chicago.

But while Torrio had managed to avoid publicity for the most part, Capone was hardly ever out of the headlines as his successor. He gradually came to symbolize all the criminal evils of prohibition and to many people throughout the world he also became the symbol of a country getting the reputation of the most lawless nation on the face of the earth. Some Americans, for a time, seemed to ignore the savage murders and vicious crimes Capone commanded, and to look upon him as something of a folk hero, akin to the colorful bad men of the Old West.

Always a talker, too much for his own good, Capone tried to present that picture of himself to reporters. "I make my money by supplying a public demand," he claimed. "If I break the law, my customers, who number hundreds of the best people in Chicago, are as guilty as I am. The only difference between us is that I sell and they buy. Everybody calls me a racketeer. I call myself a businessman. When I sell liquor, it's bootlegging. When my patrons serve it on a silver tray on Lake Shore Drive, it's hospitality."

His customers, of course, did not mix murder with their drinks, and their business wasn't the terrorizing of a city. Almost any line of business that made a profit became prey for the Capone mobs. Bakers, barbers, electrical workers, garbage men, shoe repairers, tailors, plumbers, garbage haulers, window cleaners, milk salesmen and those in some sixty other trades all paid a monthly tribute in the form of "protection money," just to be allowed to stay in business and to avoid being shot at or having their places wrecked or bombed by Capone gangs. By intimidation, force and terrorism, he kept most of the city services in line. Tradesmen passed along the costs of Capone extortion to consumers and protection racketeering added an estimated $136,000,000 to the bills Chicago people had to pay each year.

Capone began to bask in his publicity and to play up to the image of himself that some newspapers created in calling him "the big fellow" and writing of his sordid activities as if they were acts of daring. There were those who envied his power and money and others who were thrilled by the wickedness that surrounded him. People clamored for a glimpse of Capone in his $30,000 bulletproof car and the bodyguard who sat next to him with a submachine gun across his lap. In awe, they watched the procession of touring cars filled with armed hoodlums that accompanied him as he drove from his office to his lavish town house.

The cost of his "private army" was enormous, and he also paid millions of dollars to police and political fixers, and to government officials high and low, but he always had enough cash on hand to carry up to fifty thousand dollars at a time in his pockets. For amusement, he frequently bet almost that much on a roll of dice or a horse race, and he tipped lavishly. During an evening on the town, he might hand a thousand dollars to a singer who pleased him, five hundred to a hat-check girl, fifty to a passing panhandler and a five-dollar bill to a newsboy. He once said he had "fooled away" more than seven million dollars.

Capone contributed freely to the campaign funds of his

political friends. In one campaign alone, to help elect a mayor he wanted in office, he provided a quarter of a million dollars. His gang supplied men for election boards, delivered repeat voters and helped to count the ballots. When other devices failed, Capone took the more direct action of sending armed mobsters into the voting districts to use force to produce the vote as promised. Officials, in return, not only kept hands off Capone's bootlegging operations, but also ignored his other rackets. Citizen complaints often produced official statements that all the reports of crime in Chicago were "just newspaper talk."

"He was . . . bigger than the city and bigger than the state," Paul Sann wrote in *The Lawless Decade*. "He was the Mayor, Governor and Machine Boss all rolled into one. He gave the orders; the people's elected servants carried them out and kept their mouths shut. Capone's iron rule embraced not only Chicago but whatever other parts of Illinois he had the time and inclination to exploit. His authority was so great it could not be measured."

But the measure of violence at the height of the Chicago gang wars reached a murder a day, and there were bombings on an average of twice a week. Rival gangsters made at least a dozen attempts to kill Capone. The most spectacular attack, by those who had taken over the old O'Banion mob, came on the afternoon of September 20, 1926. An armed convoy of eleven touring cars, reportedly ordered into action by O'Banion's successor, Hymie Weiss, roared into Cicero.

Streets were crowded with shoppers as the gunmen began their bombardment of the inn that served as Capone's headquarters. Rolling slowly past the entrance, they opened up with pistols, sawed-off shotguns and machine guns. Capone and one of his bodyguards, who were having lunch inside, threw themselves to the floor at the sound of the first blast. More than one thousand shots were fired. The woodwork and doors were splintered, windows were shot out, upholstery was shredded and the lobby was left in ruins. Bullet holes were later found in thirty-five cars parked nearby and a woman seated in one of them was wounded by stray bullets and flying glass. Capone's bodyguard was hit in the shoulder and slightly injured, but nobody was killed. Capone picked himself up off the floor, dusted off his expensive suit and, when Cicero's friendly police came to ask about the shooting, he said, "What shooting?"

That was about as far as any investigation ever got. Several weeks later Weiss paid for the raid on Capone's headquarters by being shot to death, and a series of other killings followed. Another leader, Bugs Moran, eventually took over what had been O'Banion's gang and set up head-quarters in a garage on Chicago's North Clark Street.

There, on St. Valentine's Day in 1929, five members of the Moran gang and two friends of the gangsters were waiting for a liquor shipment from Detroit. A big black touring car pulled up, but it looked more like a police car than one that had come to deliver liquor. There was a gun rack behind the front seat and an alarm bell on the running board. Passers-by saw four men get out, two of them dressed in police uniforms, while another man, also in police uni-form, remained at the driving wheel.

Moran, taking a shortcut through an alley from his nearby home, reportedly saw the car, decided a police raid was under way and went back home. He thus escaped what apparently was meant to be his execution. The four men from the car strode into the garage, whipped open their overcoats, and produced two sawed-off shotguns and two machine guns. They disarmed the Moran gangsters and their friends, lined them up against the red brick wall of the garage with their hands over their heads and massacred them with sweeping bursts of gunfire.

Playing out their deadly charade of pretending to be policemen who were making an arrest, the two gunmen in civilian clothes came out of the garage with their hands up, followed by the two gunmen in police uniform, who acted as if they were taking the first two into custody. They got into the waiting car and drove away. When the real police finally arrived, they found six bodies. One man was still alive, but he died a few hours later in a hospital, insisting until the end that it was the police who had carried out the mass killings. Almost everybody else, including Moran himself, suspected Capone's gang.

The entire nation was shocked by the cold-blooded murders that came as an awful climax to all the other killings. People who had tolerated violence as part of prohibition's price for maintaining the liquor supply began to have serious second thoughts. Citizen groups and crime commissions started to organize. Newspapers turned to attacking Capone as a symbol of national evil. The killings of a crime reporter and an assistant state attorney added heat to public opinion. Capone soon was branded "Public Enemy Number One."

Many gang lords in other cities also began to turn against him and to demand that he be removed as Chicago's underworld boss. He had talked too much, gained too much notoriety, created too much publicity and drawn the attention of the whole country to gang activities, and they feared another outburst like the St. Valentine's Day Massacre. Instead of keeping the rackets running smoothly in Chicago, Capone had kept them in violent upheaval. Criminal syndicates that had been built through the prohibition years in other cities wanted to protect their profitable liquor operations and rackets from disruption by rivalries that might shake apart the alliances that held organized crime together. Capone was still boss, and a powerful one, but he also had powerful enemies.

While the public sense of outrage grew, and the gang bosses conspired, Capone was basking in the sun in Florida at his twenty-five-room vacation villa, attending prize fights and other public functions as an honored guest, posing for photographs with sports champions and theatrical celebrities and giving out interviews in which he complained that people had no reason to turn against him simply because he had made good in his line of business.

Early in May, 1929, the nation's gang leaders called a conference in Atlantic City, and Capone went north to attend. Top gangsters from Philadelphia, Boston, New York and other cities were there, along with some thirty delegates representing all the important Chicago gangs. Reportedly they all agreed upon a treaty, dividing the country into territories each would respect. Chicago also was divided into new areas of gang control, and the wars there were declared at an end. But Capone personally received no guarantee of his safety, and there were rumors that he was warned he would never again reach Chicago alive.

In Philadelphia, on the way back to Chicago, he was arrested, and it was said that he had arranged to have himself picked up by two detectives, who met him in front of a movie theater. He readily handed them his gun, pleaded guilty to a charge of carrying a concealed weapon and drew a year's sentence in jail. "He was running away from a gang which was out to kill him," Mayor Harry Mackey said. "If he hadn't been glad to go to jail, I think he would have fought the case to the last."

Capone was quoted as saying that "I want peace, and I will live and let live. I'm tired of gang murders and gang shootings. It's a tough life to live. You fear death every moment. . . ." He protested that nobody would give him "any peace of mind" and also objected to the fact that "I am known all over the world as a millionaire gorilla."

In the comparative safety of jail, he waited to see how Chicago's new gangland peace treaty would work out. With time off for good behavior, he was released on March 17, 1930, and left Philadelphia. But he found he was no longer anybody's hero in Chicago. Warned that officials, aroused by the public, had put twenty-five policemen on duty around his home with orders to arrest him on sight, he decided to go instead to his headquarters in Cicero. He spent four days catching up on business and then, accompanied by his lawyers, visited each of Chicago's law enforcement offices to find out what charges there were against him. Federal authorities, the state attorney's office and local police were unable to produce a single formal complaint. Since nobody had a warrant for his arrest, the police watch was withdrawn from his home.

But in Washington, prodded by President Hoover himself, the Treasury Department was determined to put Capone in prison—if not for the many more serious crimes charged to his gangs, then for violating the income tax laws. Treasury men checked books and records seized in Chicago raids over a period of years, and agents posing as hoodlums infiltrated the Capone gang. They collected enough evidence to put two of his top lieutenants in jail on tax charges, and Capone had his lawyers offer to settle his tax claims for four million dollars. But the Treasury Department was not willing to make any deals.

Capone was indicted for evading taxes, and the Department of Justice then brought five thousand separate indictments against him for bootlegging. Tried on the tax cases in October, 1931, he was found guilty and sentenced to eleven years in federal prison. He served time first in Atlanta and then in Alcatraz, and with time off for good behavior was released in January, 1939. His eight years behind bars were spent in daily fear for his life, and he came out of prison broken in health and died at the age of forty-eight in 1947.

Although it probably was the last thing he would have wished, Al Capone had done more than anyone else to arouse the nation against prohibition's gangs and to stir a deep and lasting revulsion among the people. None of the other troubles the Eighteenth Amendment had brought had so dramatically spelled out its failures as mob control of the cities and sudden death in the streets. The drys might argue with good reason that the old saloons had produced organized crime, but nobody had so clearly shown America its evils as Al Capone, brought to power by prohibition.

14

The opponents of prohibition were weakly organized at first. They lacked real leadership, funds, spokesmen and influence. Most of them thought it would be impossible ever to repeal the Eighteenth Amendment, so their first demands were for a change in the Volstead Act to permit legal beer and wine. It was six years after the start of prohibition before any strongly organized demand was made for outright repeal.

But while the drys settled back to defend prohibition against all criticism, the wets became the new crusaders and reformers. Dry organizations suffered a falling off of interest and of funds, but the wets began to rally support to fight the evils of prohibition, its lawlessness, corruption and criminal gangs.

The Association Against the Prohibition Amendment grew to be the central group around which the wet opposition gradually formed. Its strength increased year by year until it rivaled the power and effectiveness of the dry Anti-Saloon League. Other groups also gained impressive followings, and as the battle turned to one for full repeal they had the support of such national organizations as the American Federation of Labor, the American Legion and the American Bar Association.

By the end of the 1920s the national directors of the Association Against the Prohibition Amendment included more than two hundred of the richest and most powerful men in America—top directors of banks, insurance companies, automobile manufacturing concerns, railroads, communications systems and other mammoth corporations. Many wealthy men backed repeal because they wanted to cut their taxes, since prohibition was costing the federal government an estimated loss of one-half billion dollars a year in liquor revenues, replaced mainly by income taxes. But men of property also feared the growing national lawlessness, and on a profit level alone felt that repeal would bring greater gains for business.

Captains of labor, like those of industry, were finding a wide gap between the promises and realities of prohibition. Labor leaders who had backed prohibition to improve conditions of the working class saw few changes in slums, poverty or reduced drinking. Racketeers were disrupting legitimate union activities, confronting unions with strike-breaking, coercion and strong-arm tactics.

There were lawyers who felt prohibition had put such an impossible burden on the courts that it was threatening the whole legal system. Educators deplored prohibition's effects on the nation's youth. Writers, artists and other intellectuals protested that prohibition invaded individual liberties. Other opponents charged that it violated state's rights. Some claimed the dry movement was a front for racial and religious bigotry and resented the active interference of churches in political affairs. For hundreds of reasons, noble or selfish, the new crusaders gained support against prohibition from men in a position to influence others.

Women, who had always taken the leadership in the fight for prohibition, also began to organize against it. It was a crushing blow for the drys when the socially prominent wife of a New York banker, Mrs. Charles H. Sabin, called together a meeting of sixteen friends in 1929 to form the Women's Organization for National Prohibition Reform. Within three years it had more than one million members. She resigned her position as the first woman member of the Republican National Committee to head the new group, which quickly attracted other prominent women to local leadership across the country. A far cry from the hymn-singing women who led the old dry crusaders, the new reformers reflected the age of feminine independence. Led by fashionable women whose activities gained newspaper publicity, funds and a membership following, they made the repeal movement socially acceptable. They helped destroy the political myth that all women, and therefore one-half of the country's eligible voters, automatically would vote dry.

Backed by almost unlimited funds, the wet propaganda machine moved into high gear, and the drys tried to match it. No other national argument ever flooded the country with so many books, pamphlets, reports, surveys, news releases and speeches. One New York newspaper alone published more than seventeen thousand separate items dealing with prohibition in an eight-year period, and the whole United States became obsessed with talking about it until most other problems were overshadowed.

Just as the drys had before them, the wets hired well-known writers to produce supposedly impartial articles for magazines, and used economic pressure on publishers and editors to get favored treatment in newspapers. Trick by trick, they imitated what the drys previously had done in lobbying, political maneuvering and spending freely to buy influence. Much of what was said by both sides was nonsense. They dreamed up statistics, made surveys to fit their own purposes, called each other liars and matched conflicting statements by eminent economists, sociologists, political scientists, experts on courts, prisons, taxes, commerce and child welfare. Few Americans knew what to believe, and most people grew weary of the whole debate.

Public opinion polls showed a trend toward modification of the Volstead Act, if not for full repeal. The groundswell seemed even stronger in eight highly populated states where there was direct voting on liquor laws in 1926. Wets won more than fifty-nine per cent of the ballots. But the drys still held firm political control of most of the country and were able to maintain large majorities in both houses of congress until the very end of prohibition.

The battle over continued prohibition first came to a head politically in the 1928 presidential election. Drys were bitterly opposed to the Democratic candidate, New York's Governor Alfred E. Smith, an outspoken foe of prohibition and also of the Anti-Saloon League. Although Smith asked only for modification of the Volstead Act, and not for outright repeal, he had made it clear that he considered prohibition unconstitutional, undemocratic and in violation of both state's rights and individual liberties.

To many drys, whose greatest political strength rested in predominantly Protestant small towns, Smith seemed the essence of all they detested. A gravel-voiced, cigar-smoking son of an immigrant Irish teamster, he was a product of the big-city slums and had made his political home in Tammany Hall, which drew its support from the melting pot of the foreign-born. As Governor of New York for eight years he had put through much progressive and liberal legislation that had brought him into battle with ultraconservatives. Added to everything else in the minds of the prejudiced was the fact that he also happened to be a Roman Catholic.

Methodist Bishop James Cannon, Jr., chairman of the Anti-Saloon League's political activities and recognized leader of the drys following the death of Wayne Wheeler, went to the Democratic National Convention in Houston in June, 1928, with the knowledge that he had no real chance to block Smith's presidential nomination. But he used the threat of opposition to get a strong dry plank in the party's platform, which pledged the party and its nominees to "an honest effort" to enforce the Eighteenth Amendment and "all laws enacted persuant thereto."

Smith, however, refused to sidestep the issue. In his telegram of acceptance he made it plain that whatever the platform said, he was a wet. Although he agreed to run on the platform as adopted and to enforce the law if elected, he took the position that changes in prohibition laws were necessary and that it was the duty of a chosen leader of the people to point the way. The Volstead Act, he declared, should be modified.

His stand split the party. Cannon denounced Smith's message as "an action of brazen political effrontery" and led a bolt of Southern Democrats out of the convention. He announced that he and other dry leaders would throw their support to the Republican candidate, Herbert Hoover, who had declared himself against repeal or modifying the laws to enforce prohibition.

Bishop Cannon set up headquarters in Richmond, in his home state of Virginia, where he was political boss, and directed an anti-Smith campaign in fourteen Southern and border states, devoting his full time and a lot of money to seeking Smith's defeat. Although Cannon later denied he was responsible for it, the dry campaign in the South soon became identified with attacks on Smith's religious faith and open appeals to prejudice that left a deep scar on the nation's conscience.

Virulent anti-Catholic pamphlets were distributed by the thousands, intolerance was openly voiced by drys in public speeches and a well-organized rumor machine began producing bigot-frightening tales to the effect that if Smith became president the East Wing of the White House would be reserved as the American residence of the Pope and that only Catholics would hold high government jobs. There were equally scurrilous lies about Smith's character and personal habits, and false whispers that he was a drunkard or worse.

Eight Southern and border states went Republican in November, five of them in the so-called solid South, and in some of them Democrats lost for the first time in history. But nobody could really say how much effect religion and prohibition had on the outcome. Hoover's national victory was overwhelming, 444 electoral votes to Smith's 87, and other issues were more important. The idol of millions, wartime humanitarian and able Secretary of Commerce under two presidents, Hoover was credited by many as the Great Engineer and Master Builder of America's ever-swelling prosperity. He promised even better times ahead, and probably no Democratic candidate could have beaten him in the boom year of 1928.

But it was, at least in part, a great victory for the drys. They had not only defeated their leading opponent, but had won dry majorities in most state legislatures and had increased the number of dry senators and representatives in Washington. In the new Senate there would be a dry majority of 80 to 16 and in the House, 328 to 106. The Anti-Saloon League immediately called the election a popular referendum in which the nation had voted overwhelmingly in favor of continued prohibition.

Yet in state and congressional races, as well as in the presidential election, people had voted for many other reasons. What seemed on the surface a sweeping dry victory failed to reflect America's changing attitude. The bitter campaign itself had brought the Eighteenth Amendment into question, and in its aftermath demands grew more insistent, not just for modification of enforcement laws but for full repeal.

The millions of Americans who had happily voted for four more years of prosperity suffered the first of a series of shocks in the fall of 1929. In September, the stock market had reached its then all-time high. It began tapering off, and in October the market crashed. For nearly three years, stock prices declined irregularly until they had lost almost ninety per cent of their value. Business staggered, slumped and died. The boom was over, the happy days were gone and unemployment became a common disaster. The Great Depression was on, and a suddenly sobered nation was in no mood for carrying on the gay sport that had been made of prohibition.

More than anything else, the Depression finally killed the Eighteenth Amendment. Repeal might have come without it, but not so surely or swiftly. If the emotional hysteria surrounding the First World War had helped bring prohibition into being, an equal hysteria of seeking some way out of the Depression helped put it to an end. Just as the drys had once exploited patriotism to speed the passage of the Eighteenth Amendment, the wets exploited the Depression to kill it.

Every medium of print and speech was used by the wets to convince America that prohibition was the real cause of the stock market crash, business failures, joblessness and want. The drys themselves repeatedly had claimed that prohibition was responsible for the boom, and now that prosperity had collapsed the blame was turned upon them. Wets argued that legalizing liquor would create thousands of needed jobs, would produce tax money to boost declining federal funds, would end wasteful corruption and would take money from criminals and give it back to honest men. Repeal of the Eighteenth Amendment, they insisted, was a matter of national emergency.

Meanwhile, the most exhaustive study ever made of enforcement, by an official commission authorized by dry President Hoover, was about to put the detailed record of prohibition's failures before the public. One of Hoover's first acts as president had been to appoint a ten-man National Commission on Law Observance and Enforcement, headed by former Attorney General George W. Wickersham. Popularly known as the Wickersham Commission, the group collected testimony and evidence, made a careful study of the problems of prohibition for almost two years and finally reported to the president in January, 1931. The report, which filled five large printed volumes, was thorough, well documented and honest in its presentation of the facts. But it produced more ridicule than praise, and the Commission's long months of labor became a national joke.

The trouble was that its conclusions were highly contradictory. It made no major recommendations, suggested no sweeping changes and presented no clear-cut answers. In a brief general summary, signed by all the members, the Commission declared against repeal of the Eighteenth Amendment, the return of the saloon in any legalized form or modification of the Volstead Act to permit the sale of wine and beer. But the Commission found that prohibition had failed to win the support of "a very large number of respectable citizens in all communities and of the majority of citizens in most of our large cities and in several states." It said: "The Commission is of the opinion that there is as yet no adequate observance or enforcement."

Each member also made a separate statement, many of which seemed to contradict the general summary they had all signed. Two Commissioners favored repeal, seven wanted major or minor revisions of one kind or another, and only two appeared to be satisfied to leave the existing law unchanged.

When the full report reached the newspapers, there was an outcry that the whole thing was so confusing that it was meaningless. Wets interpreted it one way and drys another, and both sides were displeased. The wets thought it didn't go far enough, and the drys thought it went too far. Editorials and newspaper columns made fun of it, and cartoonists, comedians and even poets had a field day. Critics took the attitude that the Commissioners had said in one breath that prohibition was a mess and in the next that they liked it.

Whatever anybody wanted to make of it, the Wickersham report ended all pretense that prohibition had been a success. Page after page told the sorry story of its failures. Spelled out in an official document for all to read was what most Americans already knew. The Eighteenth Amendment had never been and probably never could be enforced. It might be part of the Constitution, the basic law of the land, but it lacked the power of the people behind it. In a democracy, that power still remained supreme.

15

America's beloved humorist, Will Rogers, voiced a question a lot of people were asking in 1931. "What does prohibition amount to, if your neighbors' children are not eating?" he asked. "It's food, not drink, is our problem now. We were so afraid the poor people might drink—now we fixed it so they can't eat."

With millions of Americans out of work, few were concerned with prohibition as a moral question. It had become almost entirely an economic issue, and the wets promised that repeal was the way out of the Depression. With pockets empty, homes and businesses being lost, savings gone and hunger and despair upon them, people were eager to try anything that might change the way things were. As the Depression deepened, the already strong sentiment for repeal turned into a roaring demand to sweep the Eighteenth Amendment out the door.

There were many speeches in congress on prohibition all through the fall of 1931 and the early months of 1932, but senators and representatives bottled up the question in committees and avoided putting themselves on record while they awaited the results of the coming national elections. Wets did manage one showdown vote in the House early in 1932, in a move to force action on a measure that would allow the states to decide whether to continue or to abolish the Eighteenth Amendment. The resolution was defeated 227 to 187, but wets were encouraged by the best showing they had made on a major vote since prohibition began.

The revolt broke into the open politically at the Republican and Democratic national conventions in June. President Hoover, about to be renominated by the Republicans, was ready to change his mind on prohibition, but he wanted a platform plank that would not directly commit him or his party to an outright demand for repeal. But the Republican delegates who arrived in Chicago in 1932 were in a mood far different from those of 1928. They reflected a popular revulsion against prohibition that had grown so wide and so deep that the drys were hardly heard at all.

The fight over the platform was between those who wanted the Eighteenth Amendment revised and those who wanted it flatly repealed, with no thought given to declaring that it should be kept unchanged. For twenty-four hours, the resolutions committee worked to put together a jigsaw of five hundred words that attempted to compromise conflicting views, and they finally produced a majority report that President Hoover's spokesmen approved.

It was a plank newspapers called "moist rather than dripping wet," one that gave "wets the substance of change and drys the shadow of kind words." As *Time* magazine said, "The party had pulled on rubber boots to pussyfoot its way through the campaign." Instead of specifically calling for repeal of the Eighteenth Amendment, the Republicans recommended preserving "the gains already made in dealing with the evils of the liquor traffic," but at the same time calling conventions in the states to consider a possible new amendment that would liberalize the Eighteenth. Under it, any states that so desired would be allowed to vote themselves wet. Federal laws would still prohibit saloons even in wet states, and there would be government controls to keep liquor out of states that decided to remain dry.

But the plank went on to assert that prohibition was "not a partisan political question" and that "no public official or member of the party should be pledged or forced" to support the platform if his "honest convictions" were against it. That meant all Republican candidates, as individuals, would be free to disavow the prohibition promises the party made.

The wets immediately issued a minority report, demanding that Republicans declare themselves for repeal, and carried the fight to the floor of the convention itself. Shouting delegates started a parade, marching with poles festooned with beer bottles and carrying signs that read, "We Want Repeal, No Bunk!" Somebody substituted a beer-barrel bung-starter for Chairman Bertrand Snell's gavel. The galleries burst into howling revolt as the reading of the majority report began. Snell was booed when he vainly rapped for order and reminded the gallerites they were the guests of the convention. "We're the voters!" they shouted back. "Repeal!"

On the convention floor, the heated debate went on for two hours. Senator Hiram Bingham of Connecticut led the fight for the repeal plank. "The time has come when the question must be met," he said. "All we ask is that you give the people a chance to come clear, to come clean, and not give them a plank that no one can understand. . . . We adopted the Eighteenth Amendment to win the War. Let us repeal it to win the Depression." But in the end, the Republican delegates rejected the repeal plank, 681 to 472, and went along with the majority call to liberalize the Eighteenth Amendment instead of dumping it entirely.

The Democrats who gathered in the Chicago Stadium for the start of their party convention eleven days later had been divided for months by the same argument as the Republicans, whether to come out openly for repeal or to take a less drastic stand in the interests of party harmony. At stake was the rivalry for the presidential nomination between the defeated wet crusader, Al Smith, and his former close friend, New York's Governor Franklin Roosevelt.

Smith had tried as early as March, 1931, to get the Democratic National Committee to go on record with a call for repeal of the Eighteenth Amendment. But a combination of Roosevelt men and dry Southern Democrats had blocked the move. Smith wanted to make repeal the major issue of the coming campaign, in the hope that a militant wet majority of Democrats would nominate him as the obvious candidate to fight the Republicans. But Roosevelt held that the Depression was the real issue and hoped to keep the party united behind him. Although he had been outspoken on prohibition in the past, Roosevelt was comparatively quiet on the subject in the months before the 1932 convention.

When the Democrats began arriving in Chicago, they found that Roosevelt's supporters were prepared to present a platform plank not much wetter than the moist one the Republicans had adopted. The majority of the platform committee refused at first to endorse repeal. But the mood of the convention was overwhelmingly for it and Smith was determined to carry the demand to the convention floor in a minority report. Finally the Roosevelt men withdrew their opposition, and the minority report became the plank the committee majority presented.

The call for an end to prohibition touched off a tumultuous demonstration. "We favor repeal of the Eighteenth Amendment," the Democratic pledge declared in plain words. "To effect such repeal, we demand that congress immediately propose a Constitutional amendment to truly representative conventions in the states called to act on that proposal. . . . Pending repeal, we favor immediate modification of the Volstead Act to legalize manufacture and sale of beer. . . ."

Tennessee's dry Senator Cordell Hull, soon to be Secretary of State, made an attempt to hold off the wet tide by offering the convention a minority plank that called for merely resubmitting the Eighteenth Amendment to the states. Smith, leading the stop-Roosevelt forces, had taken no direct part in the public proceedings of the convention. But Hull's speech drew him from his seat, and for ten minutes he held the spotlight and the microphone as the champion of repeal.

As far as the convention was concerned, he was fighting a cause already won, but the personal ovation for him was thunderous. To many, Smith had become a martyr in the fight against prohibition, and it was his last big moment before a Democratic convention. "If there's anything in the world today the American public dislikes, it's a dodger," he said. "The time has passed when you can be a wet among wets and a dry among drys."

It was after midnight before all the speeches were finished and the roll call began. Dry states joined wet states in demanding repeal. Delegation after delegation was swept from its old moorings. The convention gallery groaned at every dry vote, and lustily cheered every wet vote, and the delegates themselves joined in the cheering as the results were announced. By 934 votes to 213, the Democratic party had bet its political future on a flat demand for repeal.

Nominated by the convention as the Democratic presidential candidate, Franklin Roosevelt broke with tradition and flew from Albany to Chicago to accept in person. In his acceptance speech, to which he put the finishing touches aboard the plane, he told the waiting delegates, "This convention wants repeal. Your candidate wants repeal. And I am confident that the United States wants repeal." When the cheering quieted enough so he could continue, he added the words that were to echo through the whole election campaign, "From this date on, the Eighteenth Amendment is doomed!"

Four years before, the drys had been at the height of political power; but now both major parties had all but ignored them, and their only choice was between moderately wet Republicans and dripping wet Democrats. The drys called a National Conference of Organizations Supporting the Eighteenth Amendment to meet in Washington and plan strategy that would concentrate on an attempt to hold their strength in congress. They were still hopeful that President Hoover would say something friendly about the Eighteenth Amendment which would give them an excuse to support him.

But when Hoover made his acceptance speech late in August, he gave the drys little comfort. He said that while he had "always sympathized with the high purpose of the Eighteenth Amendment" and had used "every power at my command to make it effective," there was a majority sentiment unfavorable to it in "an increasing number of communities" and a spread of disrespect for law that amounted to "practical nullification" which gravely endangered the Constitution. Hoover didn't want to see the Eighteenth Amendment smashed "as by a stroke of lightning," but he felt that "a change is necessary."

The "stroke of lightning" that came in the November elections not only shattered the Eighteenth Amendment with a mandate from the people that was overwhelmingly for repeal and the rest of the New Deal but ended whatever lingering influence the drys had in the White House by making it the residence of Franklin Roosevelt instead of Herbert Hoover, and completely destroyed the last vestige of dry power to control congress.

When the same congress that had hesitated to act on prohibition before the election returned to Washington in December, 1932, to finish out its days in the "lame duck" session that would end when newly elected members and the new president took office in March, it was eager to show the voters it had turned as wet as they had. Without waiting for President Roosevelt's inauguration or the coming flood of the new congress that would soon take over, the old congress immediately went to work on measures to prime the flow of legal beer and to end the Eighteenth Amendment.

Two weeks after the session began, the House started to withdraw from national prohibition by passing a bill of its own to legalize beer by a vote of 230 to 165, after shouting itself hoarse in a six-hour debate in which forty members took to the floor. Actually the vote had no immediate effect, since the beer bill became bogged down in the Senate and would have to be revived in the next congress all over again. But for the first time in fifteen years wets had registered a majority that indicated what was to happen to the Eighteenth Amendment.

A first attempt in December to get a repeal motion through the House failed by six votes. Then, in February, 1933, came the action in the Senate on a resolution to submit a Twenty-first Amendment to the states to repeal the Eighteenth Amendment. After Senator Sheppard's dramatic but futile one-man filibuster to hold back the resolution, the Senate struck down dry attempts to channel it to state legislatures, where it would face long delays in ratification, and approved the plan called for by the Democratic platform for ratification by a simple majority vote of conventions called in each state for that purpose. There was much debate over whether congress had the power to specify, for the first time in history, that the states must use the convention method of deciding on the Amendment, but all the fine-spun legal arguments finally were brushed aside.

As the repeal resolution moved to passage in the Senate, Democratic leaders in the House called a caucus that bound its members to support repeal as a party principle. Two days after the Senate-approved resolution emerged on the House floor the final vote came, and the House sent the new Twenty-first Amendment on its way to the ratification battles in the states. Having done what its members knew the newly elected congress would have been certain to do, the old "lame duck" congress then expired and its successors, led by the New Dealers, took full command.

President Roosevelt, when he took office on March 4, 1933, also took up a personal ax to prohibition. By executive order, he chopped the funds appropriated to run the Prohibition Bureau in half and cut nearly two million dollars from the funds of the Bureau of Industrial Alcohol. He called for a copy of the Democratic platform, clipped out its promise to legalize beer, pending the full repeal of prohibition, signed his name to it and sent it to congress as a "special message" to prod action on the measure.

The whip used to drive the beer bill swiftly through the House and Senate was the government's pressing need for new tax revenue, especially to help meet the cost of emergency depression legislation. With the House voting its approval 316 to 97, and the Senate by a narrower margin of 43 to 30, the bill amending the Volstead Act was sent to President Roosevelt for his signature. Effective April 7, it authorized beer of 3.2 per cent alcoholic content by weight, imposed a five-dollar-a-barrel tax and required brewers to take out a $1,000 federal license.

"The iron hand of the brewers is again in absolute control," said the Anti-Saloon League's Francis Scott McBride. The national W.C.T.U. warned, "No nation ever drank itself out of a depression," and then added a special warning to women, "Beer makes you fat!"

But the more than two hundred breweries legally producing near-beer announced they would be ready to pour out "the real thing" ten minutes after the law took effect. The government turned its presses to high speed to produce new Internal Revenue stamps, newspapers and magazines started soliciting beer advertisements, an institute for brewmasters graduated its first class in seventeen years and expert brewers began arriving from Germany. Breweries were so swamped with applicants for work that some had to put up signs saying "No Help Wanted," and Chicago, Los Angeles, New York and other cities began issuing beer-selling licenses.

At one minute past midnight on Friday morning, April 7, 1933, a neon-lit clock in New York's Times Square began chiming "Happy Days Are Here Again!" In Washington, at the same minute, a brewery official gave the orders, "To the White House! Let her go!" With traffic cleared on Pennsylvania Avenue, a beer-laden truck rolled toward the Executive Mansion, carrying a banner that read: "President Roosevelt, The First Beer Is For You!" Aboard the truck were six Hawaiians thumping guitars, and a crowd lined the sidewalks to cheer it on its way.

President Roosevelt, who within thirty-three days after taking office had fulfilled his campaign promise to bring back beer, was asleep when the first cases were delivered to the tradesmen's entrance of the White House, but a Marine guard happily guzzled one of the bottles. Later in the morning, more cases brought by plane from breweries in Chicago and Milwaukee arrived. The president decided to donate his testimonial samples to the National Press Club.

Elsewhere across the country, beer trucks rolled freely through the streets without a necessary guard of gangsters armed with machine guns. In Manhattan a shiny brewery wagon drawn by six horses clattered to the entrance of the Empire State Building, where Al Smith stepped out to welcome its arrival. "This is surely a happy day for us all," he said. In Chicago, sirens, pistols and cowbells ushered in a zero-hour celebration that found bars dispensing to customers in rows four-deep. Brass bands paraded and steam whistles hooted at midnight in St. Louis, and by midafternoon the city had all but exhausted its first beer supply. The editor of *Brewery Age* estimated that within twenty-four hours thirsty Americans had consumed more than one and one-half million barrels of beer.

People wondered what effect the return of legal beer would have on the repeal battles getting under way in the states. Wets hoped the national beer binge would quickly subside so everybody would be convinced the country was ready to handle hard liquor with decent moderation. Drys were concerned that, with beer glasses already in hand, Americans would be more likely than ever to vote full repeal.

Michigan held the first of the state conventions during the same week as beer's return and voted three-to-one for the Twenty-first Amendment and repeal, but the Michigan results were expected. The W.C.T.U.'s Ella Boole confidently predicted that drys would be able to club down repeal in sixteen states, three more than enough to kill it. Mrs. Sabin, leading her Women's Organization for National Prohibition Reform into the state campaigns, said, "Repealists now face perhaps the hardest engagement of our great fight."

Nine states that had been expected to vote for repeal had done so by early June, but the drys hoped to make their first real showing of strength in Indiana, considered a northern stronghold of dry support. Bishop Cannon personally stumped the state at the head of a vigorous prohibition faction and declared, "If we can win here, we can prevent repeal." But Indiana voted two to one to ratify the Twenty-first Amendment, giving repeal its tenth straight victory, and the drys moved out to concentrate their campaign on the arid South.

Within another few weeks the repeal total had reached sixteen states, with none dissenting, and conventions were about to vote in the key Southern states of Alabama, Arkansas and Tennessee. "If all three agree to repeal," Postmaster General James Farley, the New Deal's political strategist, predicted, "it will be all over." President Roosevelt sent a personal message to Alabama's Democrats to urge repeal by every effort that "lies in our power."

Alabama broke the tradition of a solidly dry South by going three-to-two for repeal. By about the same kind of a vote, Arkansas carried the Twenty-first Amendment round the turn into the homestretch. In Tennessee the wets had their first bad scare, but by a very slim majority the state finally went for repeal. Far across the country in Oregon, old-time prohibition enforcer Pussyfoot Johnson said he was "plain disgusted" when that state also joined the wet parade, and he warned that the United States was in for "a five-year drunk."

Drys still thought they could find thirteen states somewhere to block repeal; but in Washington, President Roosevelt predicted the end would come before Christmas. Even the professional dry who then was in command of chasing down the nation's bootleggers, Prohibition Director Alfred Dalrymple, thought it was time to let the distilleries start planning to resume production under government license so as to be ready when repeal came. "There's no use to kid ourselves, and there isn't any use in delaying the start of liquor manufacture," he said. "It will mean putting hundreds of thousands of men back to work, and it will mean thousands of dollars of new business."

The Eighteenth Amendment's Senator Morris Sheppard had once boasted that "there's as much chance of repealing it as there is for a hummingbird to fly to Mars with the Washington Monument tied to its tail," but his own mammoth Texas became the twenty-third state to plump for repeal. Maine, which way back in 1846 had set the first state example for a prohibition law, and Vermont, which had been dry since 1852, also fell, and by mid-September only seven states stood between the Eighteenth Amendment and repeal. Virginia, in going wet, even carried Bishop Cannon's home town.

On November 7, 1933, Utah became the thirty-sixth and deciding state to vote repeal. By then the end had become so certain that Americans greeted the news with little excitement. Reporters who rushed to the law office of Andrew Volstead in Granite Falls, Minnesota, found him taking it philosophically, lounging back in his chair with his feet up on a desk. "Anything I might say could do nobody any good," he told them. "All it would do would be just to bring ridicule upon me. If I were to say that prohibition had been a mistake, there would be an awful uproar."

The formal execution didn't come until one month later, when the Utah convention met in Salt Lake City and officially ratified the Twenty-first Amendment. On December 5, at 5:32 P.M., Eastern Standard Time, having existed for thirteen years, ten months and nineteen days, national prohibition died.

President Roosevelt less than two hours later issued a proclamation to notify the country that ratification was complete and that liquor as well as beer once more was legal in the United States. "I ask the wholehearted cooperation of all our citizens to the end that this return of individual freedom shall not be accompanied by the repugnant conditions that obtained prior to the adoption of the Eighteenth Amendment, and those that have existed since its adoption," he said. "I ask especially that no state shall by law or otherwise authorize the return of the saloon either in its old form or in some modern guise."

There were some celebrations then. Here and there stuffed dummies dressed up in frock coats and battered top hats to represent the dour reformer who had come to symbolize prohibition were happily hanged from flagpoles, drowned in civic pools and fountains and shot by self-appointed firing squads of merrymakers. There were dinners, parties and in some few places repeat performances of the demonstrations that had greeted the return of beer. But for the most part, joy was more restrained, and the national reaction seemed to be a heavy sigh of relief.

Repeal did not, of course, end the Depression, although it did create an estimated one-quarter of a million jobs in the liquor and brewing industries and even more in the trades serving them. Farmers were not greatly helped since the only increased crop sales were of barley, rye and hops. But it did bring a flow of needed tax money into the national treasury and to state and city governments.

If "saloon" became a forbidden word in most places, the institution itself soon was flourishing under other names, as a cocktail lounge, tavern or grill. Before, during and after prohibition, some drinking places were high-class and some were evil joints. That had not changed.

There was a flurry of experimenting with control regulations, some of them ridiculous at first. States and cities debated whether drinkers should sit or stand, whether they should be seen from the street and if they should be served or not served, depending on whether the bartender was able to produce on demand a stale sandwich or a boiled egg that represented food and thus made the place a restaurant entitled to sell liquor. But after a time most areas settled down to sane and usually well-enforced regulations, and moderate drinking in public or private ceased to be the preoccupying obsession it had been during the years when the Twenties roared.

Alcoholism remained, as it always had been, a great and unsolved national problem and a tragedy for some individuals. But the majority of Americans seemed to look for solutions, not by drastic law, but through education, medical and scientific knowledge and moral suasion.

One unwanted heritage prohibition left the nation was a highly organized, powerful and wealthy underworld, spread across the United States in interlocking directorates of crime, grown practiced and sophisticated through years of liquor racketeering. Deprived of liquor, the gang syndicates moved into other fields where even greater profits awaited them. Among the people, too, prohibition left a disrespect for law and order, a conditioning to violence, a cynicism about government and a doubting of authority that would be long in healing.

But the Twenties also had been part of the growing up of a nation and of learning, perhaps, that there are no simple answers to complex problems. The years had begun as a time of dreaming, of wishful and noble innocence. They had ended with reality. The crash was a big one, and the landing was hard.

Suggested Further Readings

Suggested Further Readings

Asbury, Herbert, *The Great Illusion: An Informal History of Prohibition,* Doubleday & Co., Inc., New York, 1950.

Dobyns, Fletcher, *The Amazing Story of Repeal,* Willett, Clark & Company, Chicago, 1940.

Gusfield, Joseph R., *Symbolic Crusade: Status Politics and the American Temperance Movement,* University of Illinois Press, Urbana, Ill., 1963.

Krout, John Allen, *The Origins of Prohibition,* Alfred A. Knopf, New York, 1925.

Lee, Henry, *How Dry We Were: Prohibition Revisited,* Prentice-Hall, Inc., Englewood Cliffs, N.J., 1963.

Merz, Charles, *The Dry Decade,* Doubleday, Doran & Co., Inc., Garden City, N.Y., 1930.

Sann, Paul, *The Lawless Decade,* Crown Publishers, Inc., New York, 1957.

Sinclair, Andrew, *Prohibition: The Era of Excess,* Little, Brown & Co., Boston, 1962.

Walker, Stanley, *The Night Club Era,* Blue Ribbon Books, Inc., New York, 1933.

Index

Index

Index

Adams, John Quincy, 36
American Congressional Temperance Society, 36
American Society for the Promotion of Temperance, 33–34
American Temperance Union, 35
Ames, Fisher, 23
Anderson, William, 102
Andrews, Lincoln C., 127–128
Anti-Saloon League, 66, 67–71, 79, 80, 82, 85–92, 93, 94, 95, 96, 97, 99, 102, 126, 127, 128, 158, 160, 161, 162, 171
Appleton, James, 44
Association Against the Prohibition Amendment, 157, 158

Baker, Purley A., 68
Beecher, Lyman, 30–31, 33
Bingham, Hiram, 169
Blair, Henry W., 64–65
Boole, Mrs. Ella, 10, 176
Bryan, William Jennings, 72–73, 102

Cannon, Bishop James, Jr., 161, 177, 178
Capone, Al, 144–155
Celler, Emanuel, 10
Clark, Billy J., 29, 30
Colosimo, Big Jim, 143
Coolidge, Calvin, 125, 127
Curtis, Charles, 9, 10

Dalrymple, Alfred, 177
Dana, John, 46
Depression, The Great, 8, 163, 167, 179
Directions for Preserving the Health of Soldiers, 25
Doran, James M., 128
Dow, Neal, 44–46, 47, 59
Dr. Hale's Friendly Admonition to the Drinkers of Brandy, 18
Drunkard's Looking Glass, The, 32

Edwards, Edward I., 105
Edwards, Justin, 33, 35
Eighteenth Amendment. See Prohibition.
Einstein, Izzy, 131–132
Eliot, Charles, 107

Farley, James, 177
Fay, Larry, 139, 140
Fuller, Margaret, 59

George II (king of England), 18
Guinan, Texas, 138–140

Hamilton, Alexander, 22–23
Hanly, J. Frank, 88
Hannah Hawkins, or, The Re-Reformed Drunkard's Daughter, 38
Harding, Warren G., 125, 136
Hawkins, John, 38

Haynes, Roy, 127, 128
Hewitt, Nathaniel, 33
History of the Woman's Temperance Crusade, 53
Hobson, Richmond P., 88, 90
Hoover, Herbert, 154, 161, 162, 164, 168, 172, 173
Hubbard, John, 46
Hull, Cordell, 171

Inquiry into the Effects of Spirituous Liquors on the Human Body and Mind, 26, 32
Internal Revenue Act, 48

Jefferson, Thomas, 23, 24
Johnson, Pussyfoot, 72, 80–83, 177

Kenyon, William, 86
Kramer, John F., 104, 126

La Guardia, Fiorello, 10
Lawless Decade, The, 150
Lewis, Dioclesian, 51–53, 55, 59
Lincoln, Abraham, 48
Lowman, Seymour, 128

McBride, Francis Scott, 175
McCoy, Bill, 117–118
Mackey, Mayor Harry, 153
Maine Temperance Society, 44
Mitchell, William, 37
Moore, George, 76
Moran, Bugs, 151–152

Nation, Carry, 72, 76–80
Nation, David, 77
National Prohibition Party, 64, 65
National Temperance Society, 65

O'Banion, Dion, 145–147, 151
Oglethorpe, James, 17, 18, 19

Porter, Daniel, 103
Prohibition, and early America, 21–27; and Anti-Saloon League, 67–83, 85–92; and bootlegging, 117–124; and Al Capone, 143–155; and Chicago, 143–155; and Colonial America, 13–20; early days of, 101–115; and Eighteenth Amendment, 93–99; enforcement of, 125–141; and organized crime, 140–141, 143–155; fight for repeal of, 157–165; repeal of, 167–180; and smuggling, 117–124; and speakeasies, 136–141; and temperance movements, 29–40, 41–49; and W.C.T.U., 58–66; and Woman's Crusade, 51–58

Rogers, Will, 167
Roosevelt, Franklin D., 9, 170, 172, 173, 174, 175, 177, 178
Rum Row, 118–121
Rush, Dr. Benjamin, 24–27, 29, 30
Russell, Howard, 66, 87

Sabin, Mrs. Charles, 159, 176
Sann, Paul, 150
Sheppard, Morris, 9–10, 88, 93, 173, 178
Six Sermons on the Nature, Occasions, Signs, Evils and Remedy of Intemperance, 32
Smith, Alfred E., 160, 161–162, 170, 171, 176
Smith, Matthew, 37

Smith, Moe, 131–132
Snell, Bertrand, 169
Stephens, William, 19
Sunday, Billy, 72, 73–76, 101

Taft, William Howard, 87, 104
Taney, Roger, 43
Thompson, Mother, 53–54
Torrio, Johnny, 143–148
Twenty-first Amendment, 9, 11, 177, 178
Tydings, Millard, 133

Union Temperance Society of Moreau and Northumberland, 29
United States Brewers' Association, 66

Volstead Act, 97, 98–99, 105, 106, 110, 111–112, 113, 130, 134, 135, 157, 160, 161, 164, 174
Volstead, Andrew J., 97, 178

Washington, George, 21, 23, 31, 37

Webb, Eugene, 86
Webb-Kenyon bill, 87
Webster, Daniel, 36, 43
Weems, Mason Locke, 31–32
Whalen, Grover, 136
Wheeler, Wayne B., 87–88, 89, 90, 97, 103, 127, 161
Wheel Within a Wheel, A, or How to Ride a Bicycle, 62
Whiskey Rebellion, 23–24
Wickersham, George W., 164
Willard, Frances, 58–61, 62–64, 65
Wilson, Woodrow, 73, 93, 94, 99
Winthrop, John, 14
Wittenmyer, Annie, 53
Woman's Christian Temperance Union, 10, 53, 58, 60–62, 63, 64, 65, 77, 88, 102, 175
Woman's Crusade, 51–58, 59, 60, 77
Women's Organization for National Prohibition Reform, 159, 176

About The Author

BILL SEVERN, a former news editor who now devotes his full time to writing for young people, is the author of more than twenty-five books and his short stories and articles have been published in nearly one hundred magazines. Born in Brooklyn, New York, the son of a newspaper executive, he was brought up in Montclair, New Jersey, and began his writing career on a weekly newspaper on Long Island. His books include many biographies and popular social histories, as well as several devoted to the hobby of performing magic shows which he has followed since he was a boy. Among his other hobbies are American history and book collecting. He and his wife Sue, also a writer and production supervisor of a group of magazines, divide their time between an apartment in New York, where he does most of the research for his books, and a home in the Berkshire Hills of Massachusetts, where he writes them.